Effective
Soccer Goalkeeping
for Women

Tamara Browder Hageage

COACHES
CHOICE™

ISBN: 978-1-58518-638-9
Library of Congress Control Number: 2002102549

Book design and diagrams: Jeanne Hamilton
Cover design: Roger W. Rybkowski
Front cover photo: ©Scott Barbour/Getty Images
Back cover photo: Bente Skjoldager
Text photos: Rick Bennett — pages 26, 53, 84
                George Hageage — pages 38, 39
                Derek Hanson — pages 32-34, 41, 42, 44, 45, 51, 52, 54, 55,
                     57-60, 62-67, 69-71, 77, 78, 80-83, 85, 93, 95
                Patrick Woodbury — page 11

Coaches Choice
P.O. Box 1828
Monterey, CA 93942
www.coacheschoice.com

DEDICATION

This book is dedicated to all of my beautiful nieces and nephews,
Lauren, Jenna, Ashleigh, Seth Daniel, Charlie Jr., Natasha,
Eric Jr., Raymond, and my adorable godson, Michael.

In Loving Memory of
My Grandfather, Major Johnnie W. Browder Sr.
October 15, 1922 — May 21, 2001

ACKNOWLEDGMENTS

There are so many people I would like to acknowledge. Their support while I was a player and coach has enabled me to write this book. First and foremost, I would like to thank my entire family. As best as I can remember, my father rarely missed a practice or a game, all the way up until I went away to college. Thanks to my grandfather, who was, and is, without a doubt, my biggest fan. I will always be thankful beyond words to my Aunt Vera, who was like a mother to me from the age of two. Although watching me play usually made her nervous, she made me millions of wonderful dinners to keep me going and washed a lot of really dirty laundry!

I am certainly grateful to my high school coach, Oscar Abitua, for his belief in my abilities as a goalkeeper and for not labeling the position with a gender. I would like to thank Coach Brian Borde for all his technical instruction, and Coach Zdravko Popovic for his passion and high expectations for me as a player. I would like to thank Coach Gretchen Gegg for giving me my first female goalkeeper role model, and Coach Lesle Gallimore, my first female head coach, for giving me a happy ending to my college career. A sincere thank you to my coaches and managers in Denmark, Russia, and Canada, for giving me such a positive professional experience.

I would like to thank Coach Kim Shaw for infecting me with her positive coaching style and giving me the desire to be a head coach. I would also like to thank Coach Chris Knox, a dear friend, for giving me my first coaching experience as his assistant at St. Ursula High School in Toledo, Ohio; and for introducing me to Coach Rj Anderson.

I will always be grateful to Rj. As his assistant, I learned the ropes of Division I and as his friend, I received his unwavering belief in my abilities as a player, not to mention many hours of his time. In snow, rain, or humid hot weather, Rj (always in shorts I might add) made time to train with me. I will always treasure those moments as a friend and a player.

To every teammate, player, coach, and aspiring goalkeeper I had the honor of sharing the field with, I am grateful to you beyond words.

Because I have gathered so much material over the years from coaches, watching other goalkeepers, and from secondhand information, I would like to extend a sincere apology to any coach or player whose name does not appear with his or her work in reference to the goalkeeping exercises. I also apologize to anyone mentioned wrongly. With the exception of my opinions, I certainly do not claim any of the technical exercises to be my own.

A very special thanks to Mr. and Mrs. Bennett and Mr. and Mrs. Skaggs for allowing their daughters Sara Ann Bennett and Nikki Skaggs to pose for a lot of the goalkeeping photos in this book. I would also like to personally thank Mr. Rick Bennett for taking such great pictures of Sara Ann. In addition, I would like to thank goalkeepers Katie Grothkopp and Jonna Melton for taking their time to pose for many of the action pictures. A very sincere thank you to Mr. Derek Hanson for his fantastic photography and professional expertise. This book would not have been possible without you! I would like to thank Eastern Washington University for allowing me to use their facilities for the photo shoot.

I am also very grateful to Mr. Bert Zonneveld, a good friend and a wonderful man, for taking his time to write the foreword for this book. I would like to thank my super father-in-law, Dr. George Hageage Jr., for his helpful advice and honest opinions. I am of course grateful to Dr. James A. Peterson and *Coaches Choice,* for publishing my work.

Last but not least, thanks to my husband, George. Over the past 10 years I have had the pleasure of playing with him and against him on the field, and of coaching beside him at soccer camps, the Olympic Development Program, the University of Toledo, and now as his assistant at Eastern Washington University. I have grown to truly respect him as a coach and a person. Thank you so much, George, for your tremendous support, for all of the hours you spent proofreading this book, and for your insight, great ideas, and your unbelievable patience. This book would not have been possible without you, especially since it was you who gave me the idea to write it in the first place. I love you!

CONTENTS

FOREWORD

I am absolutely delighted and deeply honored to have been asked to write the foreword to this much-needed, long overdue coaching manual dealing with female goalkeepers. The reasons are simple.

First, I am an unabashed fan of the author, Tamara Browder Hageage. Sure, she writes in her acknowledgments that her grandfather is her biggest fan. Maybe so, but I must be a close second.

The second reason is the burgeoning growth of women's soccer in North America. Here we are with an unprecedented, unrivaled explosion in the number of "girls'" teams, each featuring at least one *female* goalkeeper, and nary a word about how to train and coach them.

It is an ill-kept secret that the training and coaching of goalkeepers was long neglected, even by top coaches. Only recently is more attention being paid to specific exercises and drills for this all-important position when training "the team." But what about the specific needs of a female in goal? There is not a lot out there to learn from.

I first met Tamara in Toronto, Canada, a number of years ago at a coaching clinic featuring Franz Hoek, then part of Ajax, Amsterdam, and the mentor of many world-class keepers. I was there with my son David, a full-time club head coach, to see the famous Dutchman in action.

As is often customary during these clinics, coaches in attendance will kick a ball around at lunch break. This time, however, they were in for a treat. Here was a coach, Tamara, who was willing to go in net despite the fact that the carpet-covered surface would be hard on anyone diving for the ball.

I'm sure that the first coach lining up to take his shot must have had in mind that he'd better ease up on it as this was a "mere female" in goal. However, this petite, five-foot-something "mere female" stopped his drive with ease. Likewise, many others.

I was thoroughly enjoying this fine display of goalkeeping, noticing the excellent technique this young lady used in protecting her domain, when I saw the master himself, Hoek, come back from the lunch area. Curious, he walked in the direction of the crowd that had gathered. Hoek is more than an instructor; he is an entertainer and simply loves an audience. Well, here was a ready-made audience for him.

He quickly grabbed a ball and confidently walked to the spot that the others had kicked from. There is something else you should know about Franz Hoek…he takes no prisoners.

To no one's surprise, he drove the ball with full force towards the corner of the net. It looked like a sure goal. But somehow this bundle of energy opposing him flew through the air towards the post and tipped the ball around it. The crowd applauded loudly.

Now intrigued, Hoek grabbed another ball and drove it, perhaps even harder, at goal. Same result! The crowd applauded even louder.

The battle was on! All of a sudden, an impromptu duel was in progress between Tamara and one of her idols, Franz Hoek, much to the delight of the crowd.

And that's when I became a fan of Tamara, the superb athlete that she is.

No, she didn't stop all of his shots, but stumped him often enough in the next 10 minutes to make a visible impression on the talented Dutchman. Her acrobatics to keep the ball out of her sacred area also left a real impression on my son and me.

David, who runs soccer camps in the summer, signed Tamara up as his goalkeeping instructor a few months later. And that's when I found an even more important reason to be one of her fans. This remarkable young woman is much, much more than a superb athlete. She is a superb human being as well. Warm, caring, witty, highly intelligent, well-educated, well-read, and well-spoken are just a few of the many superlatives that I could use. With her natural flair for dealing with children, she was an instant hit at the camp.

I enjoyed reading this book. You will find it extremely useful and highly informative. Every chapter is devoted to teaching you, the coach, how to teach and coach (there is a difference, you know) goalkeepers through easy-to-understand text and diagrams. Because a picture is worth a thousand words, there are a myriad of photographs included to help emphasize technique.

The book is chock-full of useful hints, reminders, and truisms. I especially like the chapters on communication and mental toughness, important enough for all players but vital for effective goalkeeping. Enjoy!

Bert Zonneveld, Youth Soccer Coach for more than 40 years
Secretary of the Georgetown Soccer Club
Georgetown, Canada

INTRODUCTION

"If my father hadn't treated me just like my brother – always telling me I was capable of the best in whatever I did – I would never have made it to the Olympic victory stand."

— Donna De Verona, Olympic Swimming Gold Medalist

The heels of your socks stick out of the backs of your shoes. The sleeves to your jersey are much too long! Your gloves, well ... you get the picture. It's not easy "fitting" in as a female goalkeeper. You learn to adjust, and you soon find yourself folding your socks just right and rolling up your sleeves to perfection. The same types of adjustments need to be made in the way female goalkeepers are trained. Unless they are 6'2" and 210 pounds, they obviously should not be trained the same way all athletes that size are trained. I feel that the never-ending battle of male vs. female in the goalkeeping arena is certainly *not* about devising two different styles of goalkeeping. It is about being realistic in respect to the physical differences, namely size and strength. Therefore, this book applies to any goalkeeper who fits this generalization. There are always exceptions.

Throughout the book I use female pronouns and focus on specific problems that arise when coaching females. However, over the past 11 years, I have used the same philosophy and techniques when coaching both male and female goalkeepers and have had equal amounts of success. The reason for choosing to direct the focus of this book on female goalkeepers is because the problems discussed are more common on the female side. I feel that this is due to pure biology and has nothing to do with ability or intelligence.

"In order to achieve excellence in all levels of the game, coaches need to operate under the premise that the demands of the game are dictated by the game, not by the sex of the athlete. Limiting or elevating your expectations of players simply because they are male or female can retard their development."[1]

Hence, in this book I will share with you some ideas on how an average 5'7", 135-pound goalkeeper can be as effective as a 6'2", 210-pound goalkeeper. Is this possible? Well, maybe not, but I hope I got your attention and interest.

From the age of 6 to age 27, from the youth league to professional ranks, I was exposed to many training methods; everything from tying my shoelaces together to diving over trash cans. I admit the trash cans were my idea, but I had nothing to do with the shoelaces! I have lived through the hard-nosed coaching styles and the "can I make you puke" drills to the all too common "you goalkeepers go over there somewhere and throw the ball to each other." It was through these many different and sometimes painful experiences that I have developed my philosophy on the goalkeeping position. I have taken all I have learned over time and tailored it to fit my size and strength as they changed and developed over the years.

My first soccer season with The Pirates, age 6

My last game as a professional with Les Dynamites de Laval, age 27

As a young girl, I had only male goalkeepers to look up to and emulate. By the time I was 13 or 14, I admitted to myself that I would never be able to move exactly like the goalkeepers I idolized. However, I never gave up my dream to be as good. This was also about the same time that I discovered a wonderful little thing called soccer camp. It was there that I met a coach by the name of Brian Borde. Through him, I learned just about everything I ever needed to know about goalkeeping, and the meaning of two very important words, technique and tactics. After a full year of trying to perfect all the many goalkeeping techniques Coach Borde taught me, I found myself getting quite frustrated with a few of them. Luckily, although I have always been stubborn, I have also always been determined. Thus, if Coach Borde's technique did not work for me, I made up my own technique that did.

Over the years, I paid close attention to all of the advice given to me from my coaches and what I picked up from watching other (mostly male) goalkeepers play. For me, the bottom line to my success was that I always tried everything that I was shown by a coach or saw while watching others play. If their advice or technique worked, great. If it didn't, I found a way that did. With that philosophy, I overcame physical barriers, knocked down many doors to all-male arenas, and endured my foot problems to the great amazement of too many foot specialists. This wonderful game has given me so much. I feel the next logical step in my career is to give as much as I can back to the game I love, and to teach what I have learned. It is my hope that this book is just the beginning.

In the following chapters, I discuss techniques on how to help your keeper handle the mental aspects of goalkeeping and the tough responsibilities of the position. In addition, I offer some helpful suggestions on how to improve a goalkeeper's ability to communicate and lead her defense on the field – in my opinion, the greatest asset of a goalkeeper. Your job as a coach will be discussed in regard to how to train and deal with your goalkeepers. Last but not least, this book covers effective goalkeeping training sessions, including technique adjustments, and numerous goalkeeping exercises.

The focus of this book is on the psychological and physical aspects faced when coaching a female goalkeeper. It will offer some instruction on goalkeeping techniques and tactics. However, this book deals more specifically with the differences that need to be addressed when coaching a female goalkeeper. My hope is that it will offer an aid in overcoming some of the misconceptions of what a female goalkeeper can and cannot do and demonstrate how to train your goalkeeper more effectively. Although I think this book could be useful to any coach regardless of the age and level of his or her keeper, this book was written specifically for the goalkeeper age 12 and above who has had instruction in basic goalkeeping techniques.

For you, the coach, the purpose of this book is to equip you with some knowledge of how to deal with your goalkeeper. She plays a very unique position, and I know it is difficult to coach 20 or so players and still find the time to meet the special needs of one or two goalkeepers. This task, I'm sure, is even more daunting if you never played the position yourself.

Although there has been tremendous improvement in goalkeeper training, the fact remains that many coaches still do not take the time to effectively train their goalkeepers. I certainly cannot claim to be the best goalkeeper or goalkeeping coach. I do, however, know what the position is all about. I have worked long and hard to obtain that knowledge. My hope is that this book can save you and your goalkeeper the trial and error I had to go through to get it.

I never made it to the Olympic stand, like Ms. De Verona, nor do I have any brothers. However, my father has always encouraged me to be whatever I wanted to be. I have spent the past 21 years of my life fighting to be an equal with men on the pitch. In this book I finally have the chance to rejoice in our *small* differences. I hope you enjoy reading it as much as I have enjoyed writing it.

[1] Jan Smisek, "Coach the Athlete, Not the Gender," *Coaching Soccer*, edited by Tim Schum, Masters Press, 1996, pg. 320

CHAPTER 1

Mental Toughness

"No one can make you feel inferior without your consent."

— Eleanor Roosevelt

Whether or not you have ever stood between the posts yourself, I am sure you have noticed how unique the goalkeeper position is. It is truly a big responsibility. No matter the size of the keeper, she has some mighty big shoes to fill. Hence, your keeper needs to be as mentally fit as she is physically fit.

On occasion, your keeper will find herself watching the ball and not participating directly in the game for long periods of time. Staying focused and "in the game" is one of the most difficult elements of goalkeeping. How many times as a coach or player have you heard about a team winning 10 to 1? In the last 20 minutes or so of the game, the goalkeeper gets caught sleeping. What about the age-old tale of a team that controlled the game for 80 minutes, took 20 shots on goal (compared to their opponent's 4), and still lost 1-0 on an "I can't believe that shot went in" goal? I know you are thinking that it is not the fault of the goalkeeper, but the offense's inability to put the ball in the back of the net. While that may be true, this book focuses on how to improve your goalkeeper, so that the best result of a game in which your forwards cannot hit the broad side of a barn will be a 0-0 draw.

SELF-CONFIDENCE

In my experience, the toughest part for the female goalkeeper, in relation to the mental aspect of goalkeeping, is the lack of self-confidence. Male goalkeepers tend to display an arrogant attitude more easily than female goalkeepers do. Even if they are no good, male goalkeepers tend to think more of themselves. Although this trait can be quite annoying, it is not all bad. Showing self-confidence when giving direction to your defense or after making a great save, even if it was pure luck, can intimidate the attacking team. It can boost your team's belief that the goal area is secure, and it can spark fear in the eyes of the attackers. When the attackers begin to doubt their abilities, the keeper has won. Intimidation can be a most effective tool for any goalkeeper at any level.

I feel it is important for coaches to impress upon their goalkeepers to try all training techniques they are exposed to, but have the courage to ultimately choose what works best for them. A goalkeeper needs to have a strong sense of self. It is imperative that they be able to confidently make quick decisions and lead their defense. This leadership ability will obviously be impossible to achieve if they cannot even make decisions for themselves.

Self-confidence, or as I like to call it, one's inner strength, is almost as impossible to coach as aggression. Players either have aggressive instincts in them or they don't. Unlike aggression, inner strength is something I believe we are all born with. Although you as a coach cannot give players their inner strength, you can help coax and lead them to it. Positive reinforcement from you every time you see a glimpse of this confidence on the field, or a few positive words when she looks like she is starting to doubt herself, will be a great help in developing your goalkeeper's inner strength. In short, like all aspects of coaching, it is all about giving direction and hoping some of it will take hold.

Mental toughness goes hand in hand with a goalkeeper's belief in herself. It is certainly not a position for the timid. Unlike a field player, who can make several mistakes in a game, when a goalkeeper makes a mistake, everybody sees it, and everybody remembers it, especially the goalkeeper. The best advice I can give any coach who has a goalkeeper who does not handle this responsibility well is to give it to her straight. If she chooses to wear the shirt, she has to accept everything that comes with it, the glory and the blame. No matter how many times you tell her that the ball went through 10 other players before it passed her, she will still feel that it was her fault. If she gets really upset but comes to practice the next day with the desire to get better, you have no worries. It is the player who dwells on it for days that you should be concerned about.

A coach named Brian Tinnion once said to me that after a loss, you can never feel too low and after a win, you can never feel too high, but as soon as the new day comes you have to start fresh. I admit that I am a very emotional person, and after a loss, I am miserable to be around. However, as we all know, you cannot let your emotions get to you during the game. If a goalkeeper makes a mistake, she must bounce right back and play twice as hard. There is no time during the game for her to feel sorry for herself. So, when should she go over the mistakes? During a game, if I was scored on, I would make a mental note of my mistake, while getting the ball out of the back of the net, and then pick my head up and focus on the game. I discovered that it was best for me to go over the whole game while warming down, when the game was still fresh in my memory. I would ask myself, what did I do well, what were my mistakes, how could I have better helped my team? I saw this emotional venting as an extremely important part of my game. To me, emotionally unwinding and reviewing what happened in a game was as important as being able to catch a ball. Without a clear head, one tends to make bad decisions. If your keeper is making bad decisions, it doesn't matter how great her hands are, because she will not be in the right position to use them!

Unlike a field player, a goalkeeper does not run up and down the field all game, exercise that helps relieve the stress and negative feelings built up during the game. Your keeper may survive a few games, but eventually she will "hit the wall" emotionally, and her play will suffer. Thus, a goalkeeper needs to learn how to deal with stress and emotions during the game and how to release them at the end of the game. Remember that it is just as helpful for her to go over the things she did well as it is to go over her mistakes. Success and failure are both habits. The latter is just the one we try to break!

I am not encouraging you to let your goalkeeper cry all over the place and carry on. I do feel, however, that it's okay to reassure her that she has the right to be mad and upset about the loss and/or mistakes she made. Encourage her to go over the mistakes in her head and learn from them. It is fine if you review them with her, but ultimately this is something she needs to be able to do for herself. No offense to coaches, but her own mistakes (and successes) will be the best coach she'll ever have. Impress upon her that when she shows up the next day for practice, she no longer has the right to carry a negative attitude. If you have to play "mean coach," so be it. I feel that by the age of 13 or 14, a young woman needs to learn to deal with and accept the responsibility of being a goalkeeper.

STAYING FOCUSED

In addition to accepting the responsibility of the position, mental toughness includes the ability to stay focused and ready for the entire 90 minutes of a game. As I said earlier, this is one of the hardest elements of being a goalkeeper. It takes a lot to brave the elements. Keeping your fingers and toes from freezing in the cold, or keeping your eye on the ball while looking into the glare of the sun, is difficult. No one can control the weather. However, you can teach your goalkeeper several things that will help her stay focused for the whole game, regardless of the weather.

Most problems arise when you are playing a weaker team. If you are playing in a competitive match or you are the weak team, it should not be difficult for the goalkeeper to stay in the game. Focus is usually lost when your keeper does not see much action, and starts to get bored. At all levels and ages, you can see goalkeepers standing 6, 12, or even 18 yards off their line, leaning on one leg with their hands on their hips or maybe looking at their gloves instead of the game in front of them. Sound familiar? It is no wonder they get bored and lose focus. The game is being played on the other half of the field, and they don't feel connected. What's the secret to staying focused or even staying warm? Staying involved!

First things first. If your goalkeeper is only standing on her six-yard line, then you must convince her that it is practically impossible for her to get beat when the ball is on the other half of the field. Move her out slowly and let her get comfortable with the idea of being so far away from the mouth of her goal. Ideally, when the ball is in the attacking third (see Figure 1-1), she should be near the top of the "D" of her 18-yard box. Pushing up when the ball is at the other end of the field will bring her closer to the action and help her stay more involved. In addition, it will bring her closer to her last defender and allow her to communicate more effectively. It will also put her in a better position to deal with through balls, because she has cut down the space between her and her last defender. So, instead of having to deal with a potential one-vs.-one situation, she has enabled herself to come out and clear the potential breakaway with her feet.

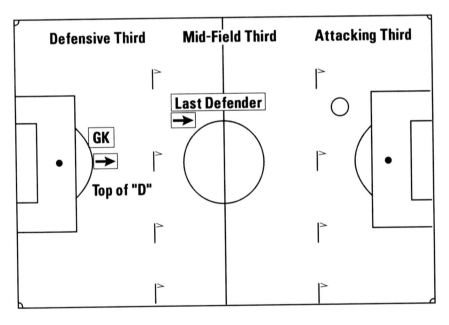

Figure 1-1.

After she gains confidence that as the ball moves closer to her she can easily move into position, you can encourage her to move with the play. This is a very simple technique. Your keeper should just follow the flow of play from side to side, as shown in Figure 1-2. This movement helped me stay warm on a cold day and kept me more focused and involved in the game.

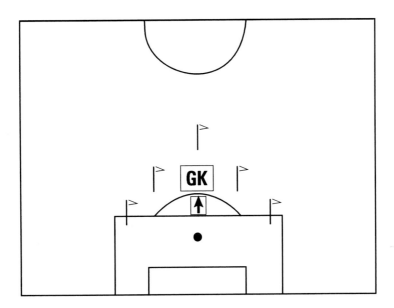

Figure 1-2. When the ball is in the attacking third, the goalkeeper should move along the flagged area in the same way a sweeper would follow the flow of the game.

Another way to stay involved is cheering on the team. Some goalkeeper coaches don't encourage this, believing that it is unnecessary noise and that if the keeper talks too much, the defense will tune her out. I happen to have been quite the cheerleader, and my defense never tuned out my voice. If the team is at the other end of the field and your goalkeeper cheers when her teammate makes a nice play, I don't think her teammates will get sick of her voice.

I believe that female athletes are very team-oriented, and have a need to support their teammates. I felt cheerleading in a game was a way of telling my players that I was with them and believed in them. It always gave me the feeling that we were all in this together; it was another way to express my passion for the game. I feel that cheering teammates on while they are at the other end of the field is a great way to keep a goalkeeper involved. When the action moves to her defensive third, her tone and words will naturally change, which will be discussed in Chapter 3.

As a young girl, I read that Alan Mayer, one of the many great goalkeepers to come out of Germany, stayed focused during a game by commentating the match to himself. I tried it for myself and ended up using this technique for nearly my entire career. Although I received funny looks from spectators and opponents, it worked like a charm! Many goalkeepers have told me that they talk to themselves or even sing their favorite song. Whatever works. It's not important what your goalkeeper does to stay focused on the game in front of her, as long as she does something. Anything is better than leaning on one leg with her hands on her hips, staring off into space, or picking at the foam on her gloves.

In essence, the combination of inner strength and mental toughness is vital to being a good goalkeeper and should be trained as such. It is a combination goalkeepers need to draw on every day of their careers.

CHAPTER 2

The Responsibility of the Coach

"Coach us the same, but treat us differently."

— Mia Hamm

The words of Mia Hamm say it best. You can expose your female keepers to the same tactical and technical situations you use with your male keepers; however, the way you treat them needs to be different. It is no great secret that most female athletes want, deserve, and expect to be treated with respect. Harsh words and silly mind games will usually backfire.

WORD CHOICE

Female athletes tend to focus on creating and maintaining friendships and value the true sense of the word "team." If you have ever coached high school girls, you have probably witnessed this "bonding" craze. If it is something that is important to them, it should be important to their coach. It is often said that the goalkeeper is not like any other player on the team, she is "special," or has to be a bit "off" to play that position. However, she is just like her teammates in regards to the importance of friendships and bonding. Even though she needs to accept the responsibility of the position and coaches need to give it to her straight, word choice is key. I do not think verbal abuse is productive when coaching any athlete, but I know from experience as a player and a coach that it will *not* be productive when coaching females.

I was brought up in the "old school" coaching philosophy of hard-nosed verbal abuse. While I responded well to this style initially, I learned very quickly, once I started competing in college and again when I started coaching, that cruel words are not productive. I know that I will not get the results that I am looking for if I choose to treat the players harshly.

The greatest coaches I've had the pleasure of working with were not necessarily great players. They did, however, have an excellent understanding of the game and, more importantly, they could communicate effectively. If you want to impress upon your goalkeeper that she must be a leader on the team and take control of her defense, you can't just get in her face and carry on about how she needs to get her head out of her you-know–where, or how she is letting everyone down. That's not to say that you have to tiptoe around the subject and its importance by sugarcoating everything. Say something like, "I have seen you play better, I realize that you cannot always be brilliant, but we all need you to be effective back there." Or you could say, "Your team needs you to talk more, our defense is in bad shape, and I know you can keep them right."

THE IMPORTANCE OF FIELD SKILLS

Coaches can never overemphasize the importance of your goalkeeper being competent on the field. During normal practice sessions, do not pair up your goalkeepers as partners. If neither of them is competent on the field, they will not be able to help each other improve. Don't think that you always have to have normal-size goals so you have a place to put your keepers during practice. Put them on the field. They could probably use the conditioning. Try to make a point at every practice to let your goalkeepers work on their field skills.

I believe the better the goalkeepers understand the field and the limits and options of each position on the field, the better equipped they will be to read the flow of the game and make sound tactical decisions. With a better understanding of the game, they will be able to anticipate possible goal-scoring situations quicker. This will allow them to better communicate to their defense in an effort to stop a possible goal-scoring opportunity. Being the ideal leader and communicating to stop goal-scoring opportunities before they develop into shots on goal *is* great goalkeeping. If your goalkeeper can learn to do this to perfection, she will not have to make brilliant saves. Your keeper's ability to communicate well with her defense can always be improved. This factor will be discussed further in Chapter 3.

GOALKEEPER TRAINING

Goalkeeper training is not just putting your keeper in the goal and doing shooting drills at her for 30 minutes to an hour. That is nonsense. Most shooting drills are designed for strikers. Most shooting drills put little or no pressure on the striker, and although they always start out 18 yards away, ultimately they end up 10 to 12 yards away. In other words, the drill becomes unrealistic and unproductive. That doesn't mean that there is no benefit for your keeper. A lot of keepers love shooting drills. It is a time for them to show off their physical abilities. The point is: don't tell yourself that you work on your goalkeepers if that is all you do.

If you don't have time during practice to work the goalkeepers, or if you do not have an assistant there to help you, then take 30 minutes to an hour before or after practice. It is important that goalkeepers receive technical training at least once a week. Always try to focus on one thing, e.g., low diving or reactions, just as you would in your field sessions. Adjust the intensity of the training depending on the amount of time you have, or if you are practicing pre- or post-game. Remember: you don't have to have a fitness-frenzy session to work on goalkeeping techniques.

GOALKEEPER SUBSTITUTION

Unlike changing a field player, changing a goalkeeper during a game can cause a major disruption. The team will have to adapt to a new voice and a new form of command from the goal. If your starting goalkeeper is having a nightmare game, then of course, get her out of there. If not, it is best to use your starting goalkeeper the whole game. If she "hits the wall," "zones," "gives up a soft goal," or whatever you want to call it, then consider substitution. Unless you are coaching a recreational team or a team of players 13 years of age and under, don't get caught up in the "Sally works just as hard and her parents are always at the game" reasoning.

In college, competitive high schools, and clubs, you should have a clear understanding with your goalkeepers that once a player has the starting position, it is hers until she loses it. This will create a good competitive atmosphere during practices between your goalkeepers. You want your second-string goalkeeper to feel that at any moment she could play, so she will train and prepare for games accordingly. And if your starting goalkeeper feels the heat of competition, she will be more apt to constantly push herself to improve. This situation will only work if you have two competent goalkeepers. If not, then pep talks and encouragement may be all you can do to help your keeper get out of a slump. Even if you have two keepers who are close in talent, as a coach, you need to determine which one is better in game situations. It is your job to put the best team on the field. That being said, there is no better teacher than pure game experience, so using your second-string goalkeeper when you are comfortably ahead is definitely a good idea. This will help build her confidence in goal and test the skills she has learned in practice.

If you feel just as confident with either goalkeeper, I suggest you alternate starters by games and not by halves. Since goalkeeping relies heavily on mind-set, starting in goal after sitting through 45 minutes of a game can be difficult. However, your backup goalkeeper must stay focused, and remember that just because she does not start the game does not mean she will not get to play. All too often, you see the backup keeper with her goalkeeper shirt off, T-shirt sleeves rolled up, socializing, and not paying attention. She should be intently watching the game in front of her and thinking about what she will need to do if she gets called into the game. Before each game, remind the backup that there is always a chance that the starting goalkeeper will have a bad day or get injured, so she needs to be ready.

The way you communicate and train your keepers is vitally important. They play a unique and important position on the field, and they deserve their own time with you or a goalkeeper coach to train for their specific position needs.

CHAPTER 3

Communicating as a Goalkeeper

"Leadership is a matter of having people look at you and gain confidence, seeing how you react. If you're in control, they're in control."

— Tom Landry

Keeper, away, push-up, mark-up, contain! Simple and specific are the secrets to good goalkeeper communication. However, there needs to be a balance between simple and specific. Sometimes simple bits of information will not be effective. For example, when there is heavy traffic in front of the goal and your keeper is yelling "pick-up," this will not always get the job done. In this situation, she needs to be more specific, such as, "Kate pick up eight on left." In high-pressure situations, it is hard to get a player's attention. If your keeper only screams "pick-up," most players will assume that she is not talking to them, and the desired defensive adjustment will not happen.

A goalkeeper being too specific can also cause problems. The fewer words used, the better. The action in a game moves quickly and leaves little time for complete sentences. Have your keeper work out her choice of words with the defense to make sure they understand exactly what she means. For example, the command "contain" would be given to the defender covering the opposing player with the ball, and would tell her to hold the player and not to dive in because her covering defender is not there yet. This is a long definition for a simple, but important, word. While in high school, I played with a sweeper who was confused by the way I said "clear" and "keeper." This was easy to fix. I just stopped saying "clear" and said "away "instead. Luckily for me, I figured this out during warm-ups! After that experience, I always made sure the defense in front of me was well aware of what I was saying to them.

A goalkeeper's ability to communicate effectively is the most important skill she can possess. If your keeper can verbally direct her defense to deny all scoring opportunities, she will not have to make any heart-stopping saves, which means less gray hair for the coach. A goalkeeper needs to communicate well with her defense because she has the best view of the field. No other player can see the game as well as she can. One of a goalkeeper's most important responsibilities is to give helpful information and direction to her team. Your keeper needs to be the eyes in the backs of their heads. The goalkeeper's voice should provide a sense of confidence and comfort that everything in the defensive third is under control.

As discussed in Chapter 1, a great deal of responsibility comes along with the goalkeeping position. Your keeper's tone of voice, word choice, and actions will have a direct effect on your whole team. She must not only be a leader in the way she physically plays in games and practices, but she also needs to lead with her voice. Physical size and strength are not a major factor. Her strength of character and self-confidence will make or break her when it comes down to communicating with the team. The ability to affect changes on the field with her voice, even when she may feel scared or nervous, will save more goals for her than her hands will.

Figure 3-1. A goalkeeper's strength of character and self-confidence will make or break her when communicating.

TONE OF VOICE

As previously mentioned, the tone and volume of your keeper's voice can be as important as her word choice. It still amazes me to hear a pathetic cry from a keeper who comes off her line and appears to command a strong physical presence. If you are standing behind the goal during a scrimmage and can barely hear what your goalkeeper is saying, her defense definitely won't be able to hear her. As long as your goalkeeper continues trying to improve her communication skills, she will get better. Like a talented field player working on a move, she needs to work on improving her words, tone, and the strength of her voice.

Depending on where the ball is on the field, her tone of voice should change. As discussed in Chapter 1, if the ball is on the other end of the field, her cheerleader voice is just fine. At this point, most of what she says will not be heard anyway. As the ball moves into the mid-field third, she should be alert to the attacking build-up from the opposing team. She should always make sure she is in the best position, so she can communicate clearly with her last defender. This will enable her to break down potential quick transitions from the opposing side.

When the ball is in her defensive third, her verbal leadership is imperative. This is when your keeper must be most alert. Her communications should consist of useful information for her defense, such as when there is a "man-on," or if there is support or need of support. The goalkeeper needs to make sure the defense is properly marking, whether playing a zonal defense or man marking. The defender that is marking the player with the ball needs information, such as whether to contain, pressure, or force the ball right or left. As her coach, you will need to explain to her when it is appropriate to use such commands. For example, use "contain" if her player is the last defender, "take ball" if the defender has support, or "force right" (or left) depending on which side the defender has support and where the goal is located. The words can vary, as long as she and her players understand each command, and they get the job done.

STRENGTH OF VOICE

The strength of her voice should depend on the situation at hand. For instance, she would shout the word "keeper" in an aggressive way when looking at an oncoming attacker, and in a more commanding tone if her defender is chasing down a loose ball in the eighteen and she decides she wants the ball. The variation in her voice can indicate many things to teammates, such as an alert of danger or safety on defense, the need for aggression toward an attacker, encouragement for the offense, or confidence in her own abilities.

FINDING HER VOICE

At first, many goalkeepers have difficulty mustering the courage to raise their voices and lead their defense. If your keepers have this problem, start them out slowly. For example, always insist they yell "keeper" when they leave their line to come out for a cross or a one vs. one, even when practicing alone. Don't settle for a "kitten" call. Make sure they say it like they mean it. Yelling "keeper" is a must. It helps goalkeepers and the team in three ways. First, it alerts the defense that the keeper is coming out of the goal mouth, so the defense will know that they need to drop back and protect the goal. Second, when said with some force, it can be very intimidating and may buy the keeper a few seconds if the attacking player flinches. Finally, as in martial arts, it can give the keeper a boost of strength and courage. Be sure that your goalkeepers yell "keeper" the moment they decide to leave the goal for a cross or the moment they decide to go for the ball on a one vs. one.

WHAT SHOULD BE SAID

The question I get most often from coaches and goalkeepers is what should be said. As stated previously, good communication is not so much what you say, but when and how you say it. Many situations that commonly arise in the defensive third require verbal communication and leadership. Unfortunately, it is impossible to cover every situation in this book. The way each keeper communicates is a part of her personality. Thus, communication style is something that will be unique to every goalkeeper. She needs to think for herself and decide how she can best lead with her voice. The following diagrams illustrate four common situations to help you understand some of the whens, whats, and hows of general goalkeeping communication.

Situation #1

When: The moment she realizes there is a corner kick

How: In a commanding tone, loud and clear

Order of Communication:

- Organize the "defensive shell." (See Figure 3-2.)

- Organize the remaining players in a goalside-marking position.

- Once the ball is kicked, yell "keeper" if leaving the line to play the ball, or "away" if holding the line.

- Once the ball is safely away or saved, command that everyone, including the post players, push up out of the 18-yard box.

Coaching Points:

- The near post player (NP) should stand up straight with her shoulder tight on the post, facing the ball. The short player (SP) should be 10 yards from the ball and one yard in from the goal line. By organizing the near post player and short player this way, a two-player wall is created, which allows the goalkeeper (GK) to cheat forward a little. There are many opinions on how to place your post player. In my experience, this is the most effective way.

- Place the far post player (FP) one step inside the goal, because it is easier to step forward, jump, and head the ball out than to bend backwards.

- The player at the top of the six-yard box (6P) should be your strongest player in the air with her head. Of course, covering your back door (BD) is always important.

- The goalkeeper should be halfway or two-thirds of the way back in the goal, again because it is easier to step forward, jump, and save the ball than to scramble backwards.

- The goalkeeper should be in an open position, facing the field. This will give her the ability to see the whole field and to move quickly in any direction.

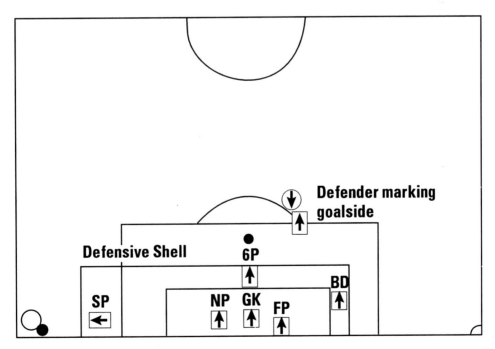

Figure 3-2. Corner kick

Situation #2

When: The moment she hears the whistle blow on a penalty

How: In a commanding tone, intense and specific

Order of Communication:

- Yell out the number of players to be used in the wall. (See Figure 3-3.) If there is no wall, then specify where the line of defense should be.

- Time permitting, quickly go to the near post and line up the post player (see NP in Figure 3-4) one step beyond the near post. This will help protect the goal from a bending ball headed for the near post.

  Helpful Hint: It is easier for your post player to face the goalkeeper and have the goalkeeper point the post player into position, instead of trying to scream over any confusion that may be going on.

- If there is an indirect kick in a dangerous position, direct the last player in the wall to act as a "bullet." (See Figure 3-4.) As soon as the ball is touched, the "bullet" player should sprint toward the ball.

- Direct the rest of the players to mark goalside and, most importantly, stay in the same line as the wall. Remember: there is offsides on a free kick.

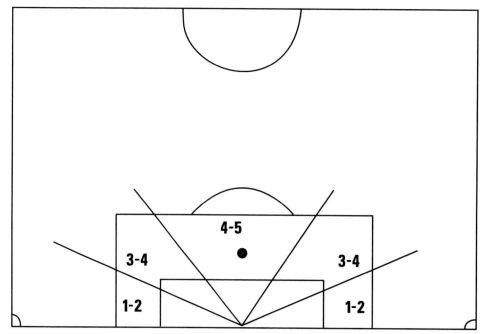

Figure 3-3. Guideline for number of players in wall

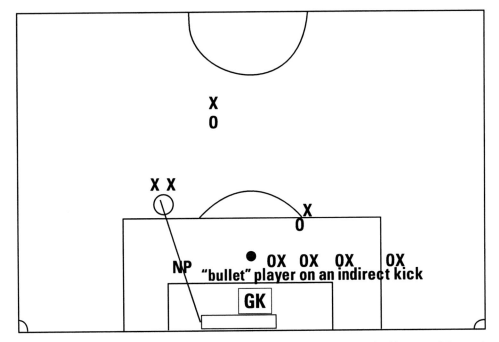

Figure 3-4. Setting a wall. Near post player (NP) is lined up half a step beyond the near post.

Situation #3

When: Once her last defender and the attacking player are within 30 yards of the goal

How: With an urgent tone, alerting to danger

Order of Communication:

- Command the last defender to contain attacker and force to the outside right or left, depending on oncoming defensive support, and whether the attacker is right- or left-footed. (See Figure 3-5.)

- Time permitting, make sure the trailing defenders are recovering.

- Encourage the defender. This can boost the defender's confidence and keep her tuned into the goalkeeper's voice and directions.

Figure 3-5. Defending a one vs. one plus
a goalkeeper

Coaching Points:

• The goalkeeper should approach the play with caution so that she stays balanced. This will enable her to react to a sudden shot or a loose ball.

• If the last defender gets beaten and the goalkeeper does not win the ball, she should stay on her feet as long as possible and continue to reduce the angle at the same pace that the attacker is moving.

• The goalkeeper has three opportunities to win the ball on a one vs. one:

❑ Smother: This can be used after the attacker touches the ball, if the goalkeeper is close enough to win the ball and the attacker dribbles the ball away from her body. This is the easiest of the three alternatives. (See Figure 3-6.)

Figure 3-6. Proper technique for smothering the ball

- ❏ Diving at attacker's feet: As the attacker is shooting, the goalkeeper dives down to the ball. Insist that she dives hands first and stays on her side. This is the most difficult and dangerous of the three options. (See Figure 3-7.)

Figure 3-7. Proper technique for diving at attacker's feet

❑ Making a wall: The goalkeeper quickly dives to the ground and makes herself as big as possible. Make sure her top arm is in front of her head to protect her face. The bottom leg should be bent slightly to ensure balance. This technique should be used as a last resort. (See Figure 3-8.)

Figure 3-8. The "wall" technique

Situation #4

When: Before and after any form of goalkeeper distribution

How: A commanding tone for organization and control

Order of Communication:

• Before distributing the ball, organize the defense according to the situation. For a long punt, drop kick, or goal kick, push players up. For any quick release, such as a throw or a pass, communicate with the receiving defender before and after distributing the ball. For example, inform the receiver to "turn" and tell her what her options are, such as if she has support to her right or has "time" to dribble. When choosing the short option, always support the throw or pass.

• After the ball is distributed, organize the defensive shape and make sure the defensive unit is stepping up with the ball.

LEADERSHIP AND YOUR GOALKEEPER

Positioned behind her teammates, your goalkeeper's leadership is essential for your team and can be the difference between a good and a great goalkeeper. Your keeper's encouragement can help your team get quickly through the letdown of a goal or help ensure focus is kept after your team scores. I've found that when playing with women, being positive and constructive is very important. If one of your defenders is upset or having a bad day, for whatever reason, it is your keeper's problem too. As the goalkeeper, she needs to do all she can to get that defender going, to let her know how much the team needs her, and to compliment and encourage her whenever possible.

The goalkeeper in soccer is similar to the quarterback in football. Like the quarterback, your keeper relies on the players in front of her. If the opponent breaks through the players in front, both the goalkeeper's and the quarterback's jobs become more difficult. So keeping the defense happy and motivated is another important aspect of the goalkeeper's long list of responsibilities.

Your keeper should talk whenever she feels it is necessary. The ability to be a strong leader and communicator in order to stop goal-scoring opportunities before they are a serious threat on goal is a large part of becoming a great goalkeeper. These are skills that can never be measured by physical size or strength, but by the size of the goalkeeper's heart and desire. These are skills that can always be improved.

CHAPTER 4

Technique Adjustments

*"You did what you knew how to do,
and when you knew better, you did better."*

— Maya Angelou

This chapter will demonstrate the flexibility and spirit in all facets of the game. In soccer, unlike many sports, there are no real "set plays," only common situations. For example, there is basically one rulebook for soccer, but every referee inevitably interprets the rules differently. The rules give referees the flexibility to exercise their views and perform in the spirit of the game. Soccer is more of a player's game than a coach's game. There are no time-outs or huddles. Once the whistle blows, it is largely up to the players to get the job done. As it pertains to goalkeeping techniques, this flexibility and spirit of the game is often overlooked. Many aspiring goalkeepers seem to get locked in a rigid world of goalkeeping drills to the point that the drill is constantly repeated, but the game is never learned. This leaves little room for the goalkeeper to exercise her own ability to find a way to the ball. Instead of using technique as an aid, practices become a never-ending drill of the goalkeeper going through the motions for the sake of technique and not the real-game situations.

PLAYING WITH LIMITATIONS

All goalkeepers have limitations. As they gain experience in their position and they get older, stronger, and hopefully wiser, their limitations may diminish, but they will never completely disappear. The word limitation has a distintcly negative ring to it.

Once we change the way we define "limitation," it will no longer be a subject that we struggle with, as a coach or a player. I like to think of the word "limitation" as simply meaning "different." Goalkeeper Brad Fidel can come off his line and take a ball in the air well above his opponent's head. I, on the other hand, have to wait until the ball is closer to the ground before I can jump to take it. This involves different timing as to when I leave my line, but also how I jump to take the ball. It produces the same result, but two different techniques are needed. Because I have a limited vertical capability, I must do things differently. A goalkeeper has to be realistic about her size. Always remember that although a tall keeper and a short keeper will have a different approach, the fundamental rules of goalkeeping still apply.

A coach who can help a goalkeeper learn to play with, not within, her limitations will be key to her success. Learning how to play with your limitations is all about knowing yourself and being completely honest about your strengths and weaknesses. As the old saying goes, "The only limitations you have are the ones you put on yourself." If you have brown hair and you want to be a redhead, then change your color. If you don't have a 40-inch vertical reach, then change your technique.

TECHNIQUE

Before we go any further, let's discuss the word "technique." It basically means how you perform a task. There are many important techniques to be learned in the goalkeeping position. They are important for two reasons. First and foremost is safety. The safety of your goalkeeper, and of all your players, should never be compromised. The second reason is to make things easier. As a coach, you should always explore different techniques that will make the goalkeeper's job easier and help her be more effective.

A good technique is one that, after it is mastered, makes a task consistently easier. If your goalkeeper cannot perform a technique, such as catching the ball with the "W" or "window," which is the technique taught by most goalkeeper coaches, it's not the end of the world. You and your keeper will just need to find a substitute technique that can accomplish the same results.

PHYSICAL PERFORMANCE

The physical performance of a goalkeeper is something that typically improves with age. However, the average female goalkeeper needs to work twice as hard as the average male goalkeeper to obtain and maintain physical strength. Adult females who are not overweight, "...have approximately 50% more fat cells than males." Therefore, it is not surprising that "...skeletal muscles in the human body...account for 40-45% of the adult male body weight and 23-25% of the adult female body weight."[1]

What does all this scientific information really mean? Nothing! Women in all sports have demonstrated how powerful they can be. Women like Billie Jean King, Jackie Joyner-Kersee, Michelle Akers, and Picabo Street, to name just a few, have changed the face of women's athletics forever.

FOUR SIMPLE ADJUSTMENTS

At this point, four simple, yet effective, technique adjustments that will help your keeper maximize her size and strength will be explained. These four examples are proof that there is always more than one way to skin a striker!

Technique #1: "The Circle"

One common physical problem for female goalkeepers is small hands and wrists. I wear a size 7 glove and have very small wrists to match. As a result, I have suffered many fractures and breaks. Hand and wrist strength is something that needs continuous attention. Lifting weights is one way to improve and maintain hand and wrist strength. Push-ups on a ball, push-ups on your knuckles, and handstands will all help increase wrist strength. Keepers should also squeeze a racket ball or use some other type of hand exerciser to strengthen their hands and fingers. Insist that your keepers perform a combination of these exercises three to four times a week. In the process, they will see marked improvement in hand strength and decrease their potential for injury.

Your goalkeeper may have strong hands but still have trouble holding on to hard-driven shots. Your first guess might be that her hands are too small, but that may not be the entire problem. If she has had any type of formal training, she probably tries to catch the ball with the famous "W" technique. (See Figure 4-1.) Many female goalkeepers should not use this technique because their hands are too small and their wrists are too weak.

Figure 4-1. The "W" technique

When I was first introduced to the "W" technique, I had a horrible time with it. After a full season of failure, I went back to my old technique, which was better suited for me. I just make a circle with my hands, with my fingers fully spread and separated at a comfortable distance, with my forearms at an angle so that there is no bend to my wrists. (See Figure 4-2.) This way, I can cover more of the surface of the ball with my hands, enabling me to use my arms more and not rely so much on my hands and wrists. Another technique, which is quite similar to the circle technique, is called the "diamond." Both these techniques are basically the same thing.

Figure 4-2. The "circle" technique

Many keepers who employ this style try to make the tips of their fingers and thumbs touch to form the "circle" or "diamond." This makes it very difficult to hold on to the ball, because the hands are too close together to get a solid grip on the ball. When instructing this technique, be sure that your keeper's fingers and thumbs do not touch. This is the problem with the "W" technique. In an effort to achieve the "strong thumbs" that make the "W" technique so successful, the keepers with small hands have to rely heavily on just two digits.

I have seen female goalkeepers who are successful with the "W" technique. The "circle" is just another option. If neither technique seems to work, your keeper may have what coaches call "hands of stone." She will need to focus on doing "soft hands" training. See Chapters 5 and 6 for "soft hands" exercises.

Technique #2: "Angle Play"

A keeper who is falling short in either jumping or diving for high shots needs to focus more on timing, timing, timing. Especially with high shots, timing is key. There is no trick to good timing; it is something that comes with a lot of practice and game experience. Keepers also need to concentrate on footwork. If they can move their feet faster, then they will not have to dive as far or jump as high to reach the ball. You and your goalkeeper should also focus on her angle play. Is she coming off her line far enough to cut off angles or is she coming out too far?

You can best explain angle play by telling your goalkeeper to visualize a line going from the posts to the ball, as shown in Figure 4-3. The closer she gets to the ball, the closer the lines get to her. Thus, a goalkeeper who stands on her goal line for a shot at the top of the eighteen has a long way to dive to each post. As she moves closer, the power dive needed at the goal line can be reduced to a reaction save.

Your goalkeeper will have to determine how far she is able to come out based on her ability to get back to cover the ground behind her. A goalkeeper who is 5'6" should be able to come out about three to four yards from the goal line when an attacker is at the top of the eighteen and has a clear shot.

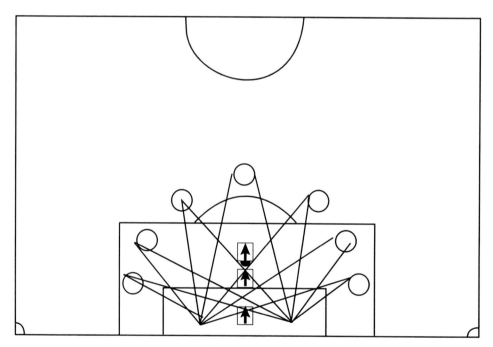

Figure 4-3. Angle play. The goalkeeper should position herself in the center of the angle. The closer she gets to the ball, the smaller her goal becomes.

Technique #3: "The Stagger-step"

The leg strength required for jumping and diving for high shots is sometimes difficult for female goalkeepers to develop. While your goalkeepers should try to improve their physical leg strength, they can also use the stagger-step technique to help alleviate the problem. (See Figure 4-4.)

The keeper staggers her feet so the foot closest to the near post is approximately 12 inches in front of the other foot. This half of a step may be all she needs to get to the ball that is just grazing her fingertips. The "stagger-step" helps in two ways. First, it gives the keeper a head start on the near-post save, which requires either kicking her feet out to make a quick reaction save, or taking a single step. (See Figure 4-5.) Because your keeper has placed her foot a step ahead, she is already halfway there, making her that much stronger and quicker. Second, when the ball is going right over her head or toward the far post, and she seems to jump too late, the "stagger-step" gives her that half-step head start.

Figure 4-4. The "stagger-step" technique

Figure 4-5. Using the "stagger-step" while making a near-post save

When you think about the footwork involved, the "stagger-step" concept becomes clearer. For example, when a high ball is going over the keeper's left shoulder, the first step for the keeper should be backwards and into the line of the flight of the ball. By having her feet staggered, her first step is already in place. The key to getting back for a high shot is remembering to take the first step back on an angle and not to waste time dropping straight back only to have to adjust sideways. This adjustment is most helpful when you are in the near-post fourth of the goal, as shown in Figure 4-6.

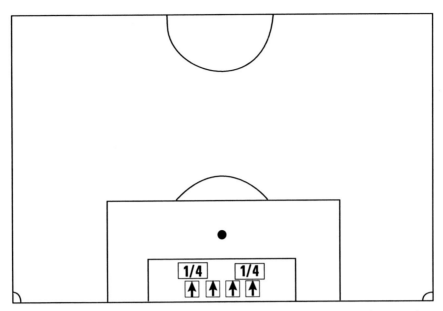

Figure 4-6. Fourths of the goal. The "stagger-step" should be used in the posts' fourths.

Over the years I have heard about and seen other techniques for saving the over-the-head, far-post shot, none of which worked very well for me. I was most successful when I kept myself square to the field with feet staggered, stayed on my feet as long as possible, and went with the opposite hand, as Figure 4-7 illustrates.

Technique #4: "Cheating in," the Lost Technique

Coming out to take a cross or to move quickly across the mouth of the goal takes fast footwork and leg strength. Most of the time, being in the right place at the right time is what it's all about. Gorden Banks, one of my favorite goalkeepers, was famous for making it look easy. With excellent footwork, angle play, and game-reading abilities, he was well-known for being in the right place at the right time.

Figure 4-8 illustrates one frequent situation and the three most common outcomes. The situation involves an attacker who dribbles the ball all the way down the flank to the goal line between the 18-yard box and the touchline. In all three scenarios, we'll assume that the attacker beats the defense. In Option A, the attacker tries for the near post. In Option B, the attacker crosses the ball. In Option C, the attacker passes the ball back to her mid-fielder, who is around the top of the 18-yard line.

Figure 4-7. Using the "stagger-step" for a far-post save

Figure 4-7. (Continued)

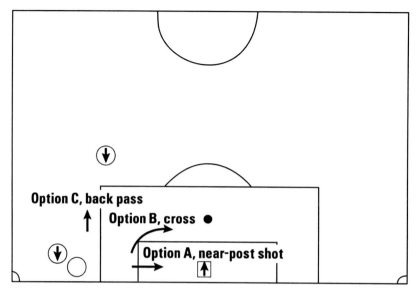

Figure 4-8. Three scenarios. In Option A, it is easier for a goalkeeper to run forward to make a save than to back up. In Option B, she will be in a better position to react to the cross, because she is in a better position to read the flight of the ball. Also, she has the room to move forward to jump. In Option C, she only needs to take two steps to get herself in the correct position for a potential shot from the top of the 18-yard box.

In all three situations, with the possible exception of the near-post shot, if the goalkeeper chooses to stick to her post, she has to scramble into position, wasting precious time. However, if she recognizes the situation and the attacker's options, she can "cheat in." When she does this, she puts herself in a better position to deal with all situations, as Figure 4-8 demonstrates. Cheating in can make her quicker and stronger and help her deal with and read the play in front of her.   If the attacker with the ball chooses to dribble closer, her angle to shoot will get better. Therefore, as the attacker moves toward the near post, the goalkeeper must also move closer to the near post.

I often see goalkeepers in a position I call post huggers. Perhaps it is a bad habit that was picked up from playing indoor soccer or watching ice hockey. Maybe this position is brought on by excessive drilling practice, and the keeper getting caught up in angle play. Your goalkeeper should never hug her post, unless she is setting up a wall or giving it a thank you kiss for saving the ball for her.

Goalkeeping rules should be used as a basic guideline; however, some will have to be adjusted to fit each individual goalkeeper. Unless the keeper is 6'2" with a terrific arm span, she cannot cheat forward and rely on her height, so she must cheat in and give herself the best angle to approach the ball and the room to move forward.

By teaching the "circle," the "stagger-step," or "cheating in," you can find ways to strengthen the abilities of your goalkeeper. If she is using a technique that isn't in any goalkeeping book, but works for her, that is great. She needs to find a way to the ball, period. As a coach, insist on good, safe techniques, but always be willing to make adjustments for what works for each individual.

[1] Sharon A. Plowman and Denise L. Smith, *Exercise Physiology for Health and Fitness, and Performance*, Allyn & Bacon, 1997, pgs. 366, 425

CHAPTER 5

Effective Training Sessions

"Lost wealth may be regained by industry. Lost knowledge by study. Lost health by temperance. But lost time is gone forever."

— Author Unknown

This chapter will offer suggestions on how to develop effective training sessions for your goalkeeper, and show you how to create your own effective goalkeeping sessions. This information will include specific examples and be divided into three parts: warm-up, focus, and fitness.

AGE AND LEVEL OF GOALKEEPER

When making up a training session, you must consider many factors, including the age and skill level of your goalkeeper. Sometimes, I find coaches who have a very talented 12-year-old goalkeeper, and train her like she is a professional. Regardless of her ability, she is only 12. Even if she is willing, and asking for more instruction, as a coach, you need to find a way to satisfy her enthusiasm, while keeping in mind that she is just a child and is still growing. Even if her parents ask you to do more, the physical and mental health of their child must always come first. To achieve this trade-off in training, give her advanced drills and situations, but modify the intensity, number of repetitions, and the amount of recovery time.

The opposite situation can also be difficult, for example, if you have a 17-year-old high school girl who has never played before. Advanced drills might only confuse her and make her over-think the position, thereby making her less effective between the posts. It is not uncommon in high school for a coach to recruit basketball or volleyball players as goalkeepers because they are tall and athletic. These athletes also need to learn all the proper goalkeeping techniques, because the position is not easy to master and without the proper training, they can get hurt or hurt someone else.

IN-SEASON VS. OFF-SEASON

Another factor to consider when you're creating a training program is the time of year, i.e., preseason, season, or postseason. Preseason is when a player can improve the most with regard to her fitness, strength, and technique. Unfortunately, this is also the time of year when you, as a coach, don't have a lot of contact with your team. Without a workout program in place, you can only hope that your players have enough discipline to exercise and stay fit. At the end of the season, tell your returning players exactly what you will expect of them when practice is resumed. Most college coaches devise an off-season workout program for their players, and many clubs and high schools are doing the same thing. If you are not sure how to plan an off-season workout for your team, contact your local collegiate, ODP, or club coach and ask for some guidance.

After the postseason break, which should not be any longer than a month, you can begin easy workouts with your goalkeepers. Continue to increase the intensity of training until a week before your first game, then taper off a bit. Just like field players, goalkeepers need some mental and physical rest to start the season fresh. Remember, goalkeeping is more mental than physical.

The intensity of regular-season training sessions should depend on your game schedule. In-season training is all about maintenance. Regular-season training is a time to focus on strengthening the areas specific to the goalkeeping position. With a game or two every week, there is no time for the in-depth style of training done during the preseason. Keep in mind that you do not have to have a shooting frenzy session, where your keeper is diving all over the place, to have an effective training session.

Pregame, the day before the match, a lot of coaches make the mistake of doing too many shooting drills. Pregame practice should be light for everyone. Basically, just do a run-through of the overall game plan and a bit of practice on set plays. Excessive shooting on your keeper can be harmful. The keeper might jam a finger or bruise a hip on the ground from a bad dive. Some coaches tell their goalkeeper not to practice at 100% to "save themselves" for the game. This is a bad idea because goalkeeping is mostly mental, and consistency is key. Asking your keeper to hold back the day before the game is a conflict of interest and can lead to bad habits and injury. If you feel your team must practice shooting, then take your starting keeper out after a while and give your backup keeper the practice. The day of the game, have your goalkeepers warm up together, do a little shooting, and then come in for corner kicks and free kicks.

Postgame is the time directly after the match and, depending on when your next match is, may or may not include the next day. Usually after a game, your keeper will feel more mentally exhausted than physically tired. Although goalkeeping during a game is very taxing on the body, it is not enough exercise to substitute for aerobic fitness. It is during the season that a keeper can lose her fitness. For example, if you have a game on Saturday, then the practice on Friday is light and Sunday is off. Depending on the intensity of the game for your keeper on Saturday, that is virtually three days off from any intense physical activity. Being in shape enough to dive around the goal and then get up the next morning is goalkeeper-fit not aerobic–fit, like a field player. Goalkeepers need to have an appropriate level of aerobic fitness. Not only will they do better in practice, more importantly, they will be better goalkeepers. They don't have to become the fastest player on the field, but because of the nature of their position, they do have to do extra aerobic conditioning on their own to keep themselves fit. The postgame time and days off are great opportunities for goalkeepers to maintain the fitness level they worked so hard to obtain during the preseason. Running for 30 minutes or performing other aerobic exercises, like swimming, or biking, are all great options for your goalkeepers to maintain their level of fitness. The postgame can also be used for more intense goalkeeping training sessions.

MAIN INGREDIENTS

The main ingredients to an effective goalkeeping session are a good warm-up, a specific focus on what is to be accomplished and worked on, and a complete warm-down. The following three sample workouts provide examples of how these ingredients could be appropriately addressed in a specific training session for goalkeepers.

WORKOUT #1

AGE: 12 LEVEL: Advanced FOCUS: Reactions

NUMBER OF GOALKEEPERS: 2

EQUIPMENT NEEDED: 8 balls, 6 cones

Figure 5-1. In-and-out footwork exercise

Warm-Up Activities:

❑ *Footwork:*

• In and out — The starting position is to the side of the cones. With a slight bend to the knees, while balancing on the balls of the feet, the goalkeeper should weave in and out of the cones, keeping her hips square, her head up, eyes forward, and hands ready. Repetitions: Up and back three times.

Figure 5-2. Up-and-over footwork exercise

- Up and over — The starting position is to the side of the cones. The leg nearest to the cone goes over first, then the second leg follows. With her knees coming up high, the goalkeeper should go up and over each cone, keeping her hips square, head up, eyes forward, and hands ready. Repetitions: Up and back two times.

Figure 5-3. Power step footwork exercise

Figure 5-4. "Set position"

- Power step — The starting position is directly facing the line of cones, one step to the side. The leg nearest the cone power-steps forward on a slight angle through the cones. The trail leg should follow but never touch the other leg. After each power step through the cones, the goalkeeper should freeze for a second in the "set position," meaning she is ready to react to a shot. Throughout the exercise, she should stay on the balls of her feet for balance, with her head up, eyes forward, knees slightly bent, and hands ready. Repetitions: Forward two times and backward two times.

Coaching notes: Footwork is a great place to start any goalkeeping session. Not only does it warm up the body, it also helps to develop coordination and balance.

❏ *Stretch*

❏ *Handwork*

- V-sits – The goalkeeper sits on the ground with her legs out in front of her, as shown in Figure 5-5. The server gives her an underhand toss to one side. The goalkeeper dives forward, trying to save the ball up toward her feet. Repetitions: Eight consecutive tosses to each side.

Figure 5-5. The technique and movements of V-sits

Coaching notes: The keeper should create a "V" when she saves the ball. She should always stay on her side and be sure her top hand is on top of the ball and her bottom hand is behind the ball. She should use the ground as a third hand. Stress the importance of letting the ball hit the ground first to cushion her fall and to pin the ball to the ground to help her hold on to it. If she keeps the ball in the air, when she hits the ground, her arms will be jarred, increasing the chance of her losing control of the ball. Also, her bottom arm should come out and away from her body. Her shoulder, not her elbow, should hit the ground first. She should keep her neck steady and straight.

V-sits help goalkeepers warm up in two ways: (1) They warm up her hands, shoulders, and neck, thus preparing her upper body for the task of diving. (2) They prepare her mentally to always attack the ball and dive toward the ball at a forward angle.

Figure 5-6. Proper technique for the strong hands exercise

- Strong hands — The goalkeeper kneels on the ground and the server strikes a ball at face or chest level. Repetitions: Two sets of 10 serves each. Serves should steadily increase in velocity.

Coaching notes: This is a great exercise to improve hand and arm strength. The kneeling position forces the keeper to use her hands and arms, instead of relying on balance and the strength of her legs.

- Pick-up — The server stands facing the goalkeeper with a ball in each hand. The server randomly drops one ball at a time, giving the goalkeeper just enough time to save the ball and toss it back to the server. The goalkeeper should not let the ball touch the ground. Repetitions: Two sets at 30 seconds each.

Figure 5-7. The pick-up exercise

❑ *Stretch*

Focus Exercises:

❑ *Exercise #1*

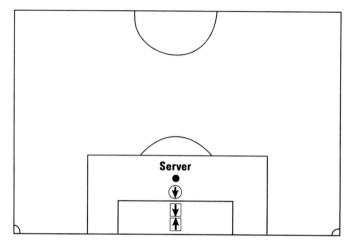

Figure 5-8

One goalkeeper faces the server. The other goalkeeper stands in front of the first (or working) goalkeeper, face to face, as shown in Figure 5-8. The two goalkeepers shuffle from post to post, passing a ball back and forth with their hands. The server randomly gives a command and then throws a waist-high ball to the side. The first goalkeeper must forget about the ball being passed and quickly react to the server's toss. Repetitions: Three sets of eight serves.

Coaching notes: The goalkeeper should try to hold on to the served ball. If she cannot hold on to the ball, she should deflect it safely around the goal post. The ball served should be thrown underhand. If served with the feet, it should be a medium-weighted pass on the ground instead of waist-high because of the close proximity and the limited reaction time.

❑ *Exercise #2*

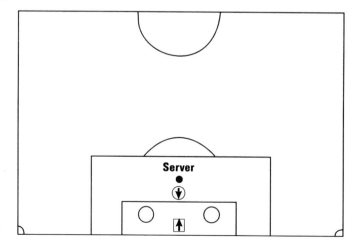

Figure 5-9

Place a ball one yard in front and one yard in from each goal post, as shown in Figure 5-9. On the server's command, the goalkeeper dives to one ball, then quickly gets up to react to the server's shot. Repetitions: Alternating each side, three sets of eight shots.

Coaching notes: Stress to the keeper to hold on to everything and to always aggressively chase down all mishandled shots. The server's shot should be between the two balls.

Warm-Down Activities:

Figure 5-10. Goalkeeper sit-ups

❑ *Goalkeeper sit-ups* — The goalkeepers lay on their backs with feet touching (see Figure 5-10). Using one ball, the goalkeepers take turns throwing the ball back and forth, doing a sit-up every time they catch the ball. Repetitions: Two sets of 25.

❑ *Push-ups.* Repetitions: Two sets of 25.

❑ *Stretch* for at least three minutes.

WORKOUT #2

AGE: 15   LEVEL: Beginner   FOCUS: Low diving

NUMBER OF GOALKEEPERS: 2

EQUIPMENT NEEDED: 4 balls, 8 cones

Warm-Up Activities:

❏ *Footwork:*

- In and out. Repetitions: Up and back three times. (See Workout #1.)

- Up and over. Repetitions: Up and back two times. (See Workout #1.)

- Rhythm – Place two cones or two balls two feet apart. The goalkeeper goes over the first cone with the leg nearest to the cone first, knees coming up high, then over the second cone. She then goes back over the second cone, then over the second cone again, back over the second cone then back over the first cone, etc. The rhythm pattern is 1, 2, 2, 2, 2, 1, 1, 1, 1, 2, 2, 2. Repetitions: Three sets of 30 seconds.

Coaching notes: Rhythm exercises will help improve your goalkeepers' timing and coordination.

Figure 5-11. The rhythm exercise

❏ *Stretch*

Focus Exercises:

❏ *Exercise #1 (Diving Circuit)*

- V-sits. Repetitions: One set of 12. (See Workout #1.)

- One-knee – The goalkeeper starts out on one knee, facing the server. The server tosses the ball underhand to the side of the keeper's raised knee. The keeper dives toward the ball, as shown in Figure 5-12.

Figure 5-12. Diving from one knee

• Standing – From a standing position, the goalkeeper performs a low dive using one step.

Figure 5-13. Diving from a standing position

Coaching notes: The primary focus should be placed on safe technique. Having the keeper start on the ground will give you the opportunity to fix problems in her diving technique before she is kneeling or standing. Things to watch for: that she stays on her side, has proper hand placement, uses the ground as her third hand, dives toward the ball at a forward angle, keeps her bottom arm away from her body (so that she is not diving on her elbow), and keeps her bottom leg slightly bent to maintain her balance. Make sure she is well-stretched before doing these exercises.

❑ *Exercise #2*

- Square exercises, set #1 – Mark off a 10-yard by 10-yard grid with four cones, as shown in Figure 5-14. The server stands in the middle of the grid. The two goalkeepers move randomly at different speeds and in different directions. On the server's command, one goalkeeper touches the nearest cone in the grid, then quickly faces the server and sets for a ball from the server. Repetitions: Eight serves to each goalkeeper.

- Square exercises, set #2 – Use the same situation described for set #1. On the server's command, one goalkeeper performs a low dive to the nearest cone, then quickly regains her feet to set for the ball from the server. Repetitions: Eight serves to each goalkeeper.

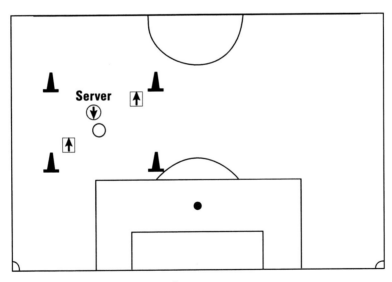

Figure 5-14. Square exercise

Coaching notes: The main focus is still safe diving technique. Make sure the serves are on the ground at a reasonable speed.

Warm-Down Activities:

❏ *Hungarian sit-ups* – The goalkeepers sit close on the ground, facing opposite directions, as shown in Figure 5-16. Interlocking hands and keeping their legs straight and off the ground, they bring their legs up and around to the other side. Repetitions: Three sets of 30.

Figure 5-15. Roll-out push-ups

❏ *Roll-out push-ups* – The goalkeeper starts out with her legs shoulder-width apart, upper body bent down, and her hands on a ball midway between her feet. (See Figure 5-15.) She rolls forward on the ball until her body is in a push-up position. She performs a push-up and then, without taking her hands off the ball or going down on her knees, she rolls back into the starting position. Repetitions: Two sets of 15.

❏ *Stretch* for at least three minutes.

Figure 5-16. Hungarian sit-ups

WORKOUT #3

AGE: 18 LEVEL: Intermediate FOCUS: Catching and throwing

NUMBER OF GOALKEEPERS: 2

EQUIPMENT NEEDED: 10 balls, 4 cones

Warm-Up Activities:

❏ *Ballwork*

Using the width of the field, the goalkeepers slowly jog, while bouncing a ball to the ground and catching it with both hands. The second time across the field, they shuffle and bounce the ball, again catching the ball with two hands.

❏ *Stretch*

Figure 5-17. Under-and-over exercise

❏ *Ball gymnastics:*

- Under and over — The two goalkeepers stand back to back, about two feet away from each other, with legs shoulder-width apart, as shown in Figure 5-17. One goalkeeper starts out with a ball. They both bend over and the one without the ball takes the ball through her legs from the other goalkeeper's hands. They then arch their backs and the goalkeeper without the ball takes the ball over her head from the other's hands. Repetitions: Two sets of 10.

Coaching notes: Make sure the players keep their eyes on the ball, always use two hands, and take the ball from each other. On the second set, have them switch roles so the one who gave the ball bending over now gives the ball arching back.

• Twist – The goalkeepers stand back to back with their legs shoulder-width apart. One has a ball in her hands. They turn to the same side and pass off the ball, then quickly turn to the other side, continuing to pass the ball off using two hands, as shown in Figure 5-18. Repetitions: One set of 20.

Figure 5-18. The twist exercise

- Extended twist – Use the same situation described for the basic twist. The goalkeepers should each take a step forward so that a space exists between them. They both turn to their right and exchange the ball in the space behind them. They then quickly turn to their left side and continue the exercise. Repetitions: One set of 20.

Figure 5-19. The extended twist

Coaching notes: These exercises are great for improving and maintaining flexibility. They also help with orientation and balance.

Focus Exercises:

❑ *Exercise #1 (Soft Hands)*

Figure 5-20. Soft hands standing exercise

- Standing – The goalkeeper starts on the goal line in a set position. The server stands in front of the goalkeeper. Using two balls is most effective, but if the server cannot perform the exercise with two balls, just use one ball. The server tosses a ball right below the goalkeeper's knee, as shown in Figure 5-20. The goalkeeper, using only the hand nearest to the ball, brings her hand out to meet the ball and then cushions the ball for control and tosses it back to the server. The server should alternate sides. Repetitions: One set of 20.

Figure 5-21. Soft hands moving exercise

- Moving – The goalkeeper again starts on the goal line in a set position with the server facing her, as shown in Figure 5-21. Using two balls, the server backs away from the goalkeeper; the goalkeeper must perform the same task described for the standing exercise, this time while moving forward. The server should go as fast as the keeper can go. Once the goalkeeper reaches the top of the 18-yard box, she should then move backward. Repetitions: One set to the top of the 18-yard box and back.

Coaching notes: Make sure the goalkeeper aggressively steps toward the ball. When she's moving backward, be sure that the goalkeeper stays balanced on the balls of her feet. Soft hand exercises are great for improving a goalkeeper's touch on the ball.

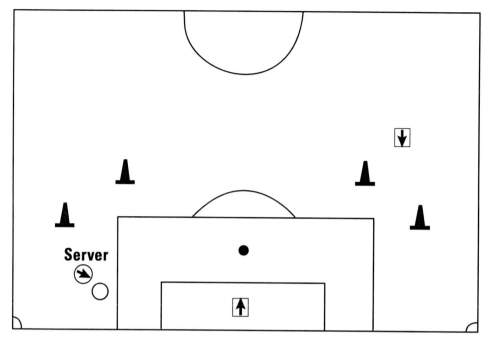

Figure 5-22. Beat the post

❏ *Exercise #2 (Beat the Post)*

Place four cones on the field as shown in Figure 5-22. The goalkeeper stands in the middle of the goal in an open position. The server throws a ball toward the near post. The goalkeeper reacts to the serve and catches the ball, ideally beyond the near post. If she catches the ball before she beats the near post, she should continue her movement until she is beyond it. Once she gains her balance, she should quickly look to the other side of the field and throw the ball between the cones so that it goes to the feet of the other goalkeeper, who is standing a few steps behind the cones. Repetitions: One set of 10 on both sides.

Coaching notes: Make sure the goalkeeper is aggressively approaching the ball and that she always tucks the ball in her arms after each catch. She should throw the ball overhand, keeping her arm straight and bringing it up around her head. (See Figure 5-23.) She should step in the direction that she is throwing, and bring her back leg forward as her arm comes around and she releases the ball. By doing this, she will maintain better balance and her throws will be more accurate. Make sure she gets her whole body behind her throw and does not just throw with her arm.

Figure 5-23. Proper technique for an overhand throw

Warm-Down Activities:

Figure 5-24. Leg scissors

❑ *Leg scissors* — The goalkeeper sits on the ground with a ball. She raises her legs about six inches off the ground and leans backward slightly to find her balance. She then weaves the ball in and out of her legs. She should keep her legs as straight as possible. Repetitions: Two sets of 50 or four sets of 25.

Figure 5-25. Manual bench press

❏ *Manual bench press* – The working goalkeeper lays flat on her back with a ball in her hands and her arms up and slightly bent. The other goalkeeper stands over her and puts pressure on the ball. The working goalkeeper resists. Repetitions: Three sets of 10 at an eight-second count.

Figure 5-26. The tuck jump

❏ *Tuck jump* – From a standing position, the goalkeeper jumps up and brings her legs into her chest. She should not pause between jumps. Repetitions: Three sets of 25.

❏ *Stretch* for at least three minutes.

All three workouts can easily be changed to fit your goalkeeper's age and skill level by adjusting the number of reps and amount of rest time. You should focus on certain techniques, depending on the level of your goalkeeper. Table 5-1 illustrates a chart that lists the basic qualities you should stress in your training sessions for each level (beginning, intermediate, and advanced). When your goalkeeper can perform all of the basic techniques in the appropriate column, you can focus on the next level.

BEGINNER	INTERMEDIATE
Fitness • Flexibility • Upper/lower body strength • Mid-section strength • Coordination training (balance orientation, reactions, rhythm, footwork)	*Fitness* • Skills listed in the beginner column • Jumping power and speed • Aerobic endurance
Technique • Competent field skills training • Catching/receiving balls high and low • Basic positioning and angle play • Diving for low balls • Distribution-punting, throwing, and bowling • Safely dealing with a one vs. one	*Technique* • Skills listed in the beginner column • Tipping over the crossbar • Boxing and catching crosses • Distribution — goal kick and drop kick • Dealing with the back pass • Power diving and diving forward
Tactics • Build confidence through safe technique • Correct only major mistakes • Do not dwell on details • Train basic communication, such as "keeper," "away," and "man-on" • Build confidence and love for the position	*Tactics* • Improve on all skills listed in the beginner column • Teach communication for leadership and better understanding of the defensive shape • Train on becoming the first line of attack and making better distribution decisions • Prepare her to maintain mental focus for entire 90 minutes • Encourage her to accept the responsibility of the position

Table 5-1. Training focal points for goalkeepers according to skill level

Patience is especially important with young women between the ages of 12 and 15. They will be going through a lot of physical and emotional changes, such as growth spurts and puberty. Because their coordination and flexibility might suffer, you should continue flexibility and strength training. In addition to physical changes, players in this age group also go through a lot of "growing pains." For example, you may notice that their priorities change from one day to the next. Again, be patient and understanding. With this age group, your parenting skills may serve you better than your coaching skills!

ADVANCED
Fitness
• Skills listed in the beginner and intermediate columns • Maximum aerobic fitness
Technique
• Skills listed in the beginner and intermediate columns • Make practice as realistic as possible to continue perfecting all techniques
Tactics
• Stress the importance of details • Train technical and tactical situations together • Improve skills listed in the beginner and intermediate columns at a more intense level (when age appropriate)

Table 5-1. (Continued)

Consistent and effective training of your goalkeeper only takes a little time, but will make a big difference for her and your team. Chapter 6 presents numerous goalkeeping exercises that can easily be plugged into the goalkeeping-training formats described in this chapter. Just like field exercises, all goalkeeping drills can be adjusted to fit the focus of your training session.

Goalkeeping Exercises

"Repetition may not entertain, but it teaches."

— Bastiat

I have been collecting goalkeeping exercises since the age of 14. My collection is a book in itself! This chapter focuses on six different areas: footwork, catching, diving, reactions, one vs. one, and crosses. In addition, this chapter includes three fun goalkeeping games that require only two goalkeepers. All the drills in this chapter can be executed with one server (a coach) and two goalkeepers. When two servers are needed, the nonworking goalkeeper is used as the other server. I hope you find the following exercises helpful. Good luck with your goalkeeping training!

FOOTWORK EXERCISES

Jumping Drills:

• *Drill #1A*

Equipment needed: 8-10 cones or balls

Place the cones or balls about one yard apart in a line. With her legs together, the goalkeeper should hop over each cone.

Coaching notes: Tell the goalkeeper to use her arms to propel her body into the air. Emphasize the height of her vertical jump, not how quickly she gets through the cones. She should land softly on the balls of her feet, which will enable her to quickly jump again without taking any extra small jumps between cones.

• *Drill #1B*

Same set-up as Drill #1A, but the goalkeeper jumps forward over two cones and then jumps backwards over one.

• *Drill #1C*

Same set-up as Drill #1A, but the goalkeeper jumps over each cone on one leg.

Coaching notes: Make sure the keeper is using not only her arms, but also her non-jumping leg to propel her body into the air. She should force her arms and the knee of her non-jumping leg up simultaneously to achieve maximum height. Make sure she lands softly on the balls of her feet.

Working time: Count going through the cones as one set. Depending on her fitness level, she could do up to three sets of each exercise consecutively.

Pattern Drills:

• *Drill #2A*

Equipment needed: Two cones

Place a cone on the six-yard box, one yard wide of each goal post. The goalkeeper starts at the right post square to the field (facing the pitch). On command, she quickly shuffles to the left post, then runs to the right cone, shuffles to the left cone, then backpedals to the right post. (See Figure 6-1.)

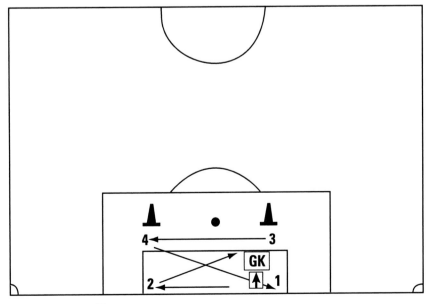

Figure 6-1. Drill #2A

Coaching notes: Her steps should be quick and smooth. She should always keep her hands in ready position. The cleats of her shoes should just glide over the grass. She should keep her head steady and her eyes forward.

• *Drill #2B*

Same set-up as Drill #2A, but begin the drill at the left post.

• *Drill #2C*

Same set-up as Drill #2A, but the goalkeeper starts at the right post square to the field, sprints to the left cone, shuffles to the right cone, then backpedals to the left post. (See Figure 6-2.)

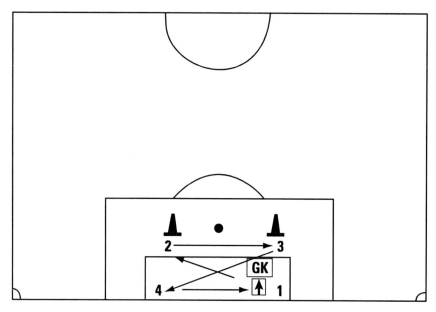

Figure 6-2. Drill #2C

• *Drill #2D*

Same set-up as Drill #2C, but the goalkeeper starts at the left post.

Working time: Set a target time to complete the circuit, 30 seconds, for example. Depending on the keeper's fitness level, rest 30, 60, or 90 seconds between each circuit.

Rhythm Drills:

• *Drill #3A*

Equipment needed: none

One goalkeeper lies on her back with her legs apart, about six inches off the ground. The other goalkeeper stands between her legs. The goalkeeper on the ground closes her legs, which will cause the standing goalkeeper to jump and spread her legs. The goalkeeper on the ground sets the rhythm for the standing goalkeeper.

Figure 6-3. Drill #3A

• *Drill #3B*

Same situation as Drill #3A, but the goalkeeper on the ground keeps her legs apart the whole time, while the standing goalkeeper quickly side steps (with high knees) in and out of her legs.

Figure 6-4. Drill #3B

• Drill #3C

Same situation as Drill #3B, but the standing goalkeeper does a two-leg hop in and out of the other goalkeeper's legs as quickly as possible.

Figure 6-5. Drill #3C

• Drill #3D

Same situation as Drill #3B, but the standing goalkeeper jumps in and out on one leg.

Working time: Use intervals of time, for example, three sets of 30 seconds.

Fast Footwork Drills:

• *Drill #4A*

Equipment needed: 8-12 cones or balls

Coaching notes: In the following exercises look for speed of execution, balance, and coordination. In each, the cones are placed in a line about two feet apart:

✓ The goalkeeper goes through the cones with high knees, then jogs back to the starting position.

✓ The goalkeeper goes through the cones with a forward shuffle then quickly backpedals to the starting position.

✓ The goalkeeper goes through the cones with a backward shuffle then quickly turns and sprints to the starting position.

Coaching notes: Unlike the "power step" discussed in Chapter 5, there is no pause between steps. She should keep her eyes forward, head steady, and hands in ready position; however, foot speed is the focus of these drills. Her steps should be quick and fluid.

Working time: Count each run through the cones and back to the starting position as one set.

• *Drill #4B*

Equipment needed: Four cones

In a 10-yard by 10-yard grid, the goalkeeper stands in the middle so the square becomes a diamond. She should always be bouncing on her toes, with her hands in ready position. Her movement is either a shuffle to the right or left, a sprint forward, a backpedal, or a jump. She should quickly respond to the following commands: right, left, up, back, or jump. At first, give her only one command at a time. As she progresses, you can give her several commands at once.

Working time: Use intervals of time, for example, three sets at 30 seconds.

CATCHING EXERCISES

Soft Hands Drills:

• *Drill #5A*

Equipment needed: One ball

Figure 6-6. Drill #5A

The goalkeeper stands with her hands at her sides. The server stands in front of the goalkeeper and holds the ball at chest height of the goalkeeper. Without notice, the server drops the ball. The goalkeeper must quickly respond and catch the ball by placing her hands on top of the ball, not under or on the side.

• *Drill #5B*

Same situation as Drill #5A, but the goalkeeper positions her hands on the side of the ball. Her hands should be a few inches away from the ball.

• *Drill #5C*

Same situation as Drill #5A, but the goalkeeper positions her hands directly above the ball. Again, her hands should be a few inches away from the ball.

Coaching notes: Having soft hands is the key to success in these exercises. If the keeper has rigid hands, she will push the ball away and will not be able to hold on to it. Remind her to relax her hands and not to snatch at the ball. If she cannot perform these exercises successfully when the ball is at chest height, then have the server release the ball at head height.

Working time: Do 8-12 repetitions. Each successful catch counts as one rep.

Shoulder Tap Drill:

• *Drill #6*

Equipment needed: One ball

Figure 6-7. Drill #6

The server stands at the side of the goalkeeper, holding the ball. The goalkeeper does not look at the server or the ball. The server gently tosses the ball so that it hits the goalkeeper's shoulder. As soon as the goalkeeper feels the ball touch her shoulder, she quickly turns and tries to catch the ball with the furthest hand from the ball. Challenge her to catch the ball as low to the ground as possible.

Coaching notes: The keeper should turn at the waist and catch the ball from underneath. As with all catching exercises, sound is the best indicator of proper technique. If there is a loud sound when she receives a ball, her hands are too rigid. Softly meeting, receiving, and cushioning the ball will produce less sound and increase the keeper's success in holding on to the ball.

Over-the-Shoulder Drill:

• *Drill #7*

Equipment needed: One ball

Figure 6-8. Drill #7

The goalkeeper stands in the middle of the goal on the goal line. The server stands about three feet from the goalkeeper. With an underhand toss, the server distributes the ball over the goalkeeper's shoulder, just above her head. Using the opposite hand, the goalkeeper receives the ball, controls it, and then tosses it back, always using just the one hand.

Coaching notes: Make sure that the goalkeeper meets the ball while it is still in front of her. She should keep her arm straight and receive the ball at the highest point.

This is an excellent drill for working on soft hands and is also a great mental exercise. In the same way that V-sits condition her to always dive toward the ball, this over-the-shoulder drill conditions her to use the opposite hand when going for a high ball. In general, when going for a low ball, her bottom hand will have the greatest reach. When going for a high ball, her top hand will have the greatest reach.

Keeper in the Middle Drills:

• *Drill #8*

Equipment needed: Four balls

The goalkeeper stands in ready position on the balls of her feet between the two servers. Each server should be about three yards away from the goalkeeper and have two balls. Using a drop kick or striking the ball from the ground, the servers alternate serves to the goalkeeper. After the goalkeeper saves a shot, she tosses the ball back to the server, then quickly turns to the other server for the next ball.

Working time: Each goalkeeper does four different sets of 12 (scoop, tuck, chest height, above head). Change goalkeepers after each set.

Figure 6-9. The "scoop" technique

Set #1 – The "Scoop"

Coaching notes: The goalkeeper should have her fingers spread with her pinkie fingers almost touching. She should come from behind the ball. If it is an easy ball to handle, she can bend at the waist. Her legs only need to be close enough together so that the ball cannot fit through. If her legs are tight together, her balance and mobility will greatly suffer. If it is a difficult ball or weather conditions are bad, she should kneel flat so that the knee of the leg furthest from the ball almost touches the heel of the foot closest to the ball. By doing this, and scooping the ball from behind, all gaps between her legs will be covered. In both techniques, she should always step through, come forward, and safely tuck the ball away in her arms.

Figure 6-10. The "tuck" technique

Set #2 – The "Tuck"

Coaching notes: When using this technique, she needs to keep her legs apart for balance. She should receive the ball with outstretched arms and cushion it by bending over. Her head should be over the ball, and her elbows as close together as possible.

Set #3 – Chest Height

Coaching notes: As discussed in Chapter 5, make sure the keeper meets the ball, and cushions and tucks each serve.

Figure 6-11. Catching the ball above the head.

Set #4 – Above Head

Coaching notes: The serve should be high enough over the keeper's head so she must completely extend her arms but not jump. Make sure that she catches the ball at the highest point and that it is far enough in front of her that she can always see it. Her wrists should be slightly bent. By doing this, if she cannot hold on to the ball, the ball will fall in front of her and give her a second chance to gain possession.

Catching and Footwork Drills:

• *Drill #9*

Equipment needed: Two cones and a small supply of balls

Make a small goal with the cones, approximately 3-5 yards wide. The goalkeeper stands in the middle of the small goal just behind the cones.

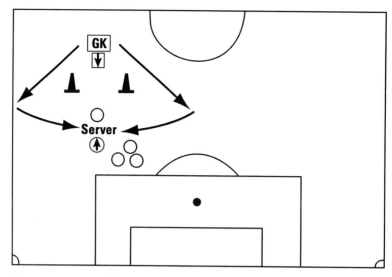

Figure 6-12. Drill #9, variation #1

Variation #1 – The server, who is about five yards away, serves a ball to one side. The goalkeeper quickly shuffles from behind the cone and then around to meet the shot. After a save is made, the keeper should quickly shuffle back to the starting position. As soon as she reaches the middle again, the server can serve the next ball to the other side.

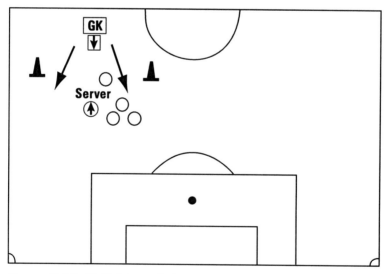

Figure 6-13. Drill #9, variation #2

Variation #2 – Same situation as variation #1, but the goalkeeper must quickly collect the ball in front of the cone.

Coaching notes: All four catching techniques (the "scoop," the "tuck," chest height, and above head) discussed in Drill #8 can be used in this exercise.

Working time: Use either intervals of time or numbered sets.

DIVING EXERCISES

Near-Post Save Drill:

• *Drill #10*

Equipment needed: One cone and a supply of balls

Place the cone three yards in from the near post and 3-6 yards out from the goal line. The goalkeeper approaches the cone, and as soon as she is in front of the cone the server directs the ball between the near post and the cone. (See Figure 6-14.)

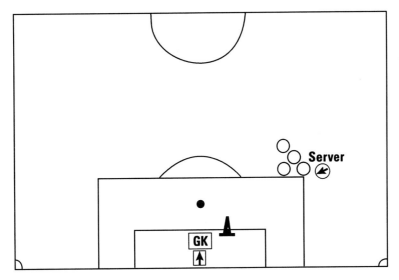

Figure 6-14. Drill #10

Coaching notes: Depending on the level and age of your goalkeeper, adjust the distance of the cone away from the goal line (the closer the cone is to the goal, the easier the exercise). Both low and high diving can be used in this exercise. Remember, if she is diving for a low ball, her bottom hand has the best reach, and if she is diving for a high ball, her top hand will have the best reach. She should always try to use two hands whenever possible.

Working time: Use sets of 8-12 repetitions. Always have the keeper train from both sides.

Diving and Footwork Drills:

• *Drill #11*

Equipment needed: One cone and a supply of balls

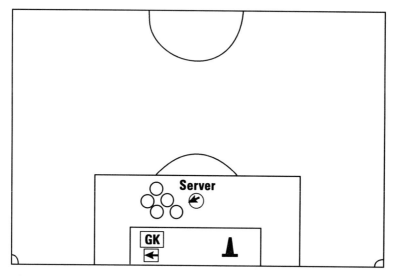

Figure 6-15. Drill #11

Variation #1 — Place the cone three-quarters of the way in from the near post on the goal line. The goalkeeper stands facing the corner flag, with her shoulder next to the near goal post. On the server's command, she quickly turns to face the field and shuffles over to save the shot. The server should aim to distribute the ball just inside the cone.

Variation #2 — Same situation as variation #1, but the goalkeeper starts the drill laying flat on her stomach with her arms outstretched. She should be at the near post, facing the corner flag.

Coaching notes: Make sure the keeper is reacting quickly to your signal and that she is using the correct number of steps. If she cannot save the shot with two hands, insist that she use a flat palm to redirect the ball out of bounds. She should always follow up any ball that is not fully saved. This drill is suitable for both high and low diving.

Working time: Use sets of 8-12 repetitions. Train both sides.

Low/High Drill:

• *Drill #12*

Equipment needed: A supply of balls

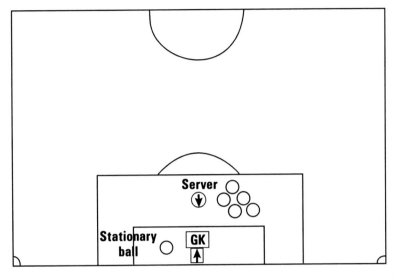

Figure 6-16. Drill #12

Place a stationary ball on the field as shown in Figure 6-16. The goalkeeper stands in the middle of the goal, about two yards out. On the server's command, she dives on the stationary ball, then quickly gets up and reacts to a high ball from the server.

Coaching notes: Learning to make combination saves is important. After making her first save, the keeper should get up without using her hands. This technique will enable her to use her hands quickly for the next shot. If she stays on her side and moves at game pace when diving for the first ball, she will have enough momentum to rock back on her legs and regain her ready position quickly. Have her practice this technique before you begin the exercise.

Working time: Perform sets of 8-12 repetitions.

Combo Diving Drill:

• *Drill #13*

Equipment needed: A supply of balls

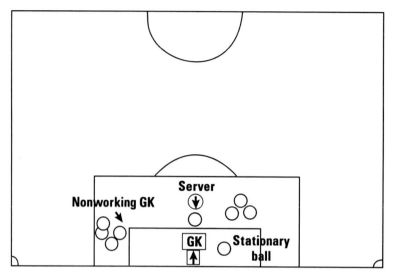

Figure 6-17. Drill #13

Arrange the field as shown in Figure 6-17, with the goalkeeper standing in the middle of the goal, about 2-3 yards off the goal line. When she is ready, she goes toward the nonworking goalkeeper to make a near-post save. She then shuffles back to the middle of the goal to save a shot from the middle server. After the second save, she quickly proceeds to dive on the stationary ball. After the third save, she again gets back to the center of her goal to take the fourth and final shot from the middle server. The four saves equal one complete repetition.

Coaching notes: This exercise is an excellent drill for testing a keeper's fitness and skills under pressure. With a high-pressure exercise such as this one, the most important task is to keep the ball out of the back of the net.

Working time: Do sets with 1-3 repetitions. Remember to change the near-post save to the other side of the goal.

REACTION EXERCISES

Shadow Diving Drill:

• *Drill #14*

Equipment needed: Two cones

Make a small six-yard-wide goal with the cones. The two goalkeepers stand facing each other on opposite sides of the goal. Pick one goalkeeper to be the leader and the other goalkeeper to be the follower. The leader makes quick movements up, back, side to side, diving to a cone, and jumping. The follower goalkeeper shadows the leader's movements.

Working time: Use intervals of time, for example, one minute. Be sure to alternate the leadership role.

Rapid Fire Drill:

• *Drill #15*

Equipment needed: 6-8 balls

Line the balls up 8-12 yards away from the goal. The goalkeeper stands in the goal, lined up with the first ball to be served. Without pausing, the server goes down the line of balls, trying to shoot each ball within one yard of the goalkeeper. The goalkeeper quickly reacts to the shots and tries to save as many as possible. The ability to get up without using your hands is of great importance in this exercise. Once all the balls are served, the set is over.

Working time: Do 2-3 sets.

Turn on Command Drill:

• *Drill #16*

Equipment needed: A supply of balls

The server stands 12-18 yards away from the goal. The goalkeeper stands in the middle of the goal with her back facing the server. On the server's command, the goalkeeper quickly turns to save a shot from the server. After making the save, the goalkeeper returns to her original starting position.

Coaching notes: The goalkeeper should always be up on her toes so she can turn and react quickly to each shot. Remind her to keep her weight on the balls of her feet so that she dives toward the ball and not backwards. Insist that she either holds on to the shot or deflects it away safely.

Forward Roll Drill:

• *Drill #17*

Equipment needed: A supply of balls

The server stands 12-18 yards away from the goal. The goalkeeper stands in the middle of the goal on the goal line. When the goalkeeper is ready, she performs a forward roll. As soon as the server can see the goalkeeper's face, the server shoots the ball directly at the goalkeeper.

Coaching notes: Make sure the keeper is not using her hands to get up. If she tucks in her head and legs and pushes off at a good pace, her momentum will bring her to her feet. Make sure she can perform this technique safely before you begin the exercise. Since you are striking the ball directly at her, insist that she holds on to the ball.

Working time: Do sets of 8-12 shots.

Football Drill:

• *Drill #18*

Equipment needed: One American football

The server stands 8-12 yards away from the goalkeeper and throws the football at the ground near the goalkeeper. The goalkeeper reacts to the bounce of the football and quickly collects the ball by scooping, diving on, or smothering the ball.

Working time: Do sets of 8-12 serves.

ONE VS. ONE EXERCISES

No Fear Drill:

• *Drill #19*

Equipment needed: A supply of balls

The working goalkeeper begins the drill up on her arms in a push-up position. A server stands on each side of her. One server passes a medium-fast ball underneath the goalkeeper. As soon as the ball passes underneath, the goalkeeper quickly drops to her side to make a wall. (See Figure 6-18.) The second server strikes the ball into the goalkeeper.

Figure 6-18. Drill #19

Coaching notes: Make sure that the keeper stays on her side, that she makes herself as big as possible, and that she keeps her top arm in front of her face. This drill is a great exercise for beginning goalkeepers because it will allow them to get a feel for the ball. It will prove to them that it is not as awful as it looks and, with the proper technique, it is not that painful. If she is a beginner, start her out with a soft shot and work up to a game-like shot. This drill is also a great warm-up activity if the focus of the session is one vs. one.

Goalkeeper vs. Goalkeeper Drill:

• *Drill #20*

Equipment needed: Four cones or two goals, and a supply of balls

Place a second goal on top of the 18-yard box so that they face each other, or use cones to make two goals 18 yards apart. Put a ball midway between the two goals. One goalkeeper stands on each goal line. On the server's command, they race out to get the ball. The goalkeeper who touches the ball first tries to score on the other with her feet.

Working time: Play the best out of 10 or use a set time of play, such as five minutes.

50/50 Drill:

• *Drill #21*

Equipment needed: 6-8 balls

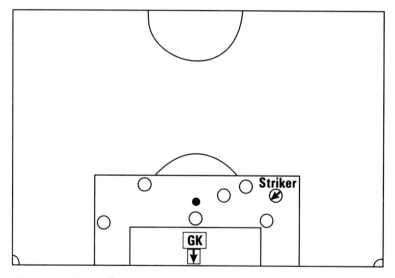

Figure 6-19. Drill #21

Place six to eight balls randomly in the 18-yard box. The working goalkeeper stands in the goal with her back to the field. The other goalkeeper acts as the striker and stands the same distance from one of the balls as the working goalkeeper does. When the goalkeeper is ready, she turns, and both she and the striker go for the ball. After the goalkeeper goes through all the balls, she becomes the striker, and the striker becomes the goalkeeper.

CROSSES ACTIVITIES

Square Work Drills:

• *Drill #22*

Equipment needed: Four cones and a supply of balls

Make a 10-yard by 10-yard grid with the cones. The server stands in the middle of the grid with the balls. The goalkeepers move randomly in the grid.

Working time: Do four different sets of 8-12.

Set #1 – On the server's command, one goalkeeper goes for the high ball.

Set #2 – One goalkeeper acts as a striker and cannot use her hands. On the server's command, both keepers go for the ball.

Set #3 – Both goalkeepers fight to catch the ball.

Coaching notes: Make sure she catches the ball at its highest point and practices going off one leg. (See Figure 6-20.) The one-leg takeoff is similar to the lay-up technique in basketball. The hands should receive the ball from behind and slightly underneath the ball. The bent leg's knee should come up high. If she just bends her leg at the knee, the leg becomes a weight and will not help thrust her into the air. The leg that comes up to the high-knee position should be the leg nearest to the attacker. Bringing up her leg helps her in three ways: (1) it helps her jump higher, (2) it is a source of protection, and (3) it will help her keep her balance. It improves balance because if the attacking player hits her while she is in the air, she will land on her straight leg (also known as the strong leg) and will easily regain her balance. If she chooses to bring up the knee furthest from the attacker, and the attacker hits her while she is in the air, she will quickly hit the ground because her strong leg will not be in position to rebalance her. Set #1 is a warm-up period to focus on proper technique. Set #2 simulates a more realistic game situation. Set #3 puts each goalkeeper in a high-pressure situation.

Figure 6-20. Catch the ball at its highest point.

Crosses and Throwing Drill:

• *Drill #23*

Equipment needed: Four cones and a supply of balls

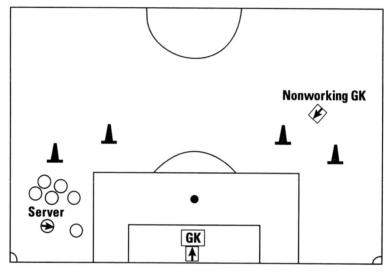

Figure 6-21. Drill #23

Set up the field as shown in Figure 6-21. The goalkeeper, in an open position, places herself two-thirds of the way back in the goal to receive the cross. As soon as she catches the ball, she quickly turns to the other side of the field and throws the ball overhand between the cones to the nonworking goalkeeper's feet. After the throw, she returns to the original starting position. Each serve is one repetition.

Variation – The nonworking goalkeeper acts as a striker and applies pressure to the goalkeeper. The goalkeeper still throws the ball through the cones.

Working time: Do 8-12 repetitions. Be sure to work both sides.

Shot/Cross Drill:

• *Drill #24*

Equipment needed: 12-16 balls

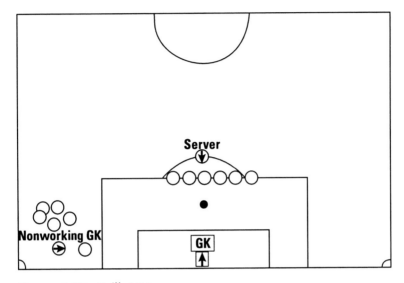

Figure 6-22. Drill #24

The goalkeeper positions herself correctly for the shot being taken by the server at the top of the 18-yard box. After she makes the save, she quickly positions herself to take a cross. The nonworking goalkeeper throws the ball between four and eight yards in from the goal line for the cross.

Coaching notes: Make sure the keeper is going to the cross and winning the ball as soon as possible, preferably toward the near-post end of the box. Stress to her that oncoming attackers will be running in, and she needs to beat them to the ball.

FUN GAMES FOR TWO GOALKEEPERS

• Game #1: Hot Pepper

Equipment needed: A supply of balls

The goalkeepers stand six yards apart, facing each other. They take turns drop kicking a ball to each other.

Rules:

✓ The goalkeeper cannot move out of the way of the kick.

✓ If the ball touches the goalkeeper and she fails to catch the ball, the other goalkeeper gets a point.

Coaching notes: If your goalkeepers have not yet mastered the drop kick, have them throw the ball at each other.

Working time: Either play for a predetermined number of drops, for example, three drops and you lose, or play for a set amount of time. The goalkeeper with the fewest drops wins.

• Game #2: Goalkeeper Wars

Equipment needed: Two goals (or four cones), a supply of balls, and two cones for midfield markers

Place the two goals about 18 yards apart. Each goalkeeper stands in a goal. One goalkeeper starts with the ball in her hands; however, they both should have a supply of balls in their goal. Divide the grid in half with two cones for the midfield markers.

Rules:

✓ Each goalkeeper must stay on her half of the field.

✓ The goalkeeper can throw, drop kick, volley, or shoot the ball to score on the other goalkeeper.

✓ If a goalkeeper makes a save and the ball is deflected into the other half, she loses possession of the ball, and the same goalkeeper gets a second shot.

✓ Once a goalkeeper has control of the ball, she may dribble up to the midfield line before she shoots.

Working time: Play to a predetermined number of goals or use a set amount of time, for example, 10 minutes.

• Game #3: Goalkeeper Golf

Equipment needed: 9-18 cones and two balls

Randomly place the cones on the field at different angles and distances. Each goalkeeper has a ball. They take turns trying to knock down a cone with a throw. They keep track of how many throws it takes to knock the cone down. After the first goalkeeper knocks down the cone, she sets it up for the other goalkeeper. The starting position for each new cone (or "hole") is the previous cone. The goalkeeper with the fewest throws (or "strokes") is the winner.

FINAL WORD

Although this book was primarily written for coaches, I would like to give a final word to all aspiring goalkeepers. My best advice to you is to always play with passion and for the love of the game!

Tamara Browder Hageage is the goalkeeper coach and assistant women's soccer coach at Eastern Washington University. She began her soccer career at the age of six. At Woodward High School in Toledo, she was a four-year starter in goal for the boys' varsity team. She was a member of the Ohio-North State Team from 1990 until 1997. She was selected to the regional team/pool from 1992 to 1997, and was invited to the national team tryouts in 1992 and 1993.

Tamara's college career began in 1990 as a scholarship athlete at Colorado College, where her team made it to the NCAA Division I Final Four. She completed her last three years of collegiate eligibility at the University of Washington, where she received MVP honors in 1991 and still holds several records, including most goalkeeper saves in a season (106 in 1991), most goalkeeper shutouts in a season (8 in 1991), and most goalkeeper saves in a match (14 vs. Michigan State, 9/23/92).

After graduating from Washington in 1994, Tamara returned to Toledo to complete a master's degree and began her coaching career by helping to lead St. Ursula High School to the regional finals. She also played on a men's semi-professional team.

In 1995, Tamara played with the Cincinnati Leopards of the Women's United States Interregional Soccer League (U.S.I.S.L) and helped the team reach the final six. In 1996 and 1997, she continued to play in the U.S.I.S.L as a captain for the Cleveland Eclipse. During this time, Tamara also worked as the assistant coach for the University of Toledo.

In 1998, Tamara headed to Russia to play for Ryazan F.C. in the Russian First Division. Next, she played for Denmark's F.C. Fortuna, one of the biggest, most successful women's professional clubs in Europe. She was the first American to sign a professional contract n the Danish First Division and the first to win the club's most valuable player award. Tamara also played professionally for Laval in Montreal, Quebec.

After retiring from professional soccer in 1999 due to congenital foot problems, Tamara was named the head women's soccer coach at Northview High School in Sylvania, Ohio. She led Northview to their highest ranking ever in the state and was named the 1999 District Coach of the Year. In July 2000, Tamara took over the women's soccer program at Eastern Washington University with her husband, George Hageage.

In 2004, Tamara earned her advanced national diploma from the National Soccer Coaches Association of America and helped lead the Eastern Eagles to a piece of the Big Sky Conference title. In the summer of 2005, Tamara was one of two athletic directors for the People to People Sports Ambassador Program and led a group of 600 players and 34 coaches in a tournament in Haarlem, Holland.

Tamara and her husband, George, have a son, George IV, who was born in January 2004. She is also the author of Effective Soccer Goalkeeping for Women, and is the featured speaker on two videos, Effective Soccer Goalkeeping for Women, Volumes 1 and 2. In addition to coaching responsibilities at EWU, Tamara focuses her professional energy on helping coaches and goalkeepers become more effective by serving as the director of coaching for the Spokane Valley Junior Soccer Association, working with the Washington State Olympic Development goalkeeping staff, and volunteering as a coach for Spokane's TOPSoccer program.